Following God

THE LEADER'S GUIDEBOOK

LIFE PRINCIPLES FROM THE PROPHETS OF THE OLD TESTAMENT

THE LEADER'S GUIDEBOOK

LIFE PRINCIPLES FROM THE PROPHETS OF THE OLD TESTAMENT

for the Bible-study workbook by

Wayne Barber

Eddie Rasnake

Richard Shepherd

AMG Publishers™
Chattanooga, TN 37422

Following God

THE LEADER'S GUIDEBOOK:
LIFE PRINCIPLES FROM THE PROPHETS OF THE OLD TESTAMENT

Published by AMG Publishers
All Rights Reserved.

ISBN: 0-89957-293-6

Printed in Canada
07 06 05 04 03 02 —T— 6 5 4 3 2

Preface

A Leader's Guide is for leaders. What does it mean to be a leader? The apostle Paul stands as one of the most noteworthy leaders in all of human history. In 1 Corinthians 3:10, Paul states, *"According to the grace of God which was given to me, as a wise master builder I laid a foundation, and another is building upon it. But let each man be careful how he builds upon it."* Upon close examination, that verse speaks volumes about leadership. As a small group leader you are building on a foundation laid by someone before you. What is the counsel of the Holy Spirit to us through the apostle Paul? What was he saying to the Corinthians that applies to us today?

First, Paul speaks of being a wise master builder. The Greek word he uses for master builder, *architekton*, is where we get our word, "architect." But *architekton* pictures more than simply the act of designing a building. It comes from two root words: *arche,* meaning "beginning," "origin," or "the person that begins something" and *tekton,* which means "bringing forth," "begetting," or "giving birth." *Architekton* carries the idea of one who leads forth, who goes first, who is the first to bring something to light. As a small group leader, you have the opportunity to guide people in the discovery of what it means to follow God. As you discuss each of the lessons and the people and concepts you will meet in those lessons, you and your group will learn some eternal truths about what it means to follow Jesus day by day.

Paul speaks of another aspect of being a Spirit-filled leader, and it is the essential work of *"the grace of God."* All Paul did, all he taught, every spiritual truth he helped others to see, was by the grace of God. It should be the same for you. You must depend on the Lord to be the Teacher for these lessons. By His Spirit, He will guide you in understanding His Word and His ways with His children. He will open the pages of Scripture. He alone knows the heart of each group member, and He alone has the wisdom you and your group need to walk through these lessons and to make the applications to daily life.

In 1 Corinthians 3:10, the Greek word for *"building"* refers to continuous, ongoing building, and pictures placing brick upon brick, stone upon stone. We are building day by day as we spend time with the Lord in His Word and obey what He is teaching us. As you walk through each lesson week after week, another stone can be added to the life of each group member, another truth can be built into each life, and another set of truths can be added to what God is doing in you as a group. Each group will be unique. Each week will be unique. The creativity and work of the Spirit of God will ebb and flow in different ways in each heart and in the group as a whole. You as a leader have the opportunity to encourage your group to be watching for the building work of the Spirit of God. Some insights will come when each is alone with the Lord. Other insights will not be seen until you come together as a group. The Spirit of God uses both means. It is a continuous adventure of discovering more about Him, His ways, and what it means to follow Him.

With this Leader's Guide, we want to come alongside and help you lead your small group in **following God** more closely and more consistently. Be a focused, attentive leader/builder. Paul said *"let **each** man be careful how he builds."* That means each of us. No one is exempt. As a small group facilitator, you will have the opportunity to lead others and experience one of the greatest times of building lives. Let us lead as *"careful"* builders, depending on the grace and the wisdom of God.

Following His leadership,

Wayne A. Barber

Eddie Rasnake

Richard L. Shepherd

Table of Contents

How to Lead a Small Group Bible Study

Causes of a Poor Study Group

The best way to become a better discussion leader is to regularly evaluate your group discussion sessions. The most effective leaders are those who consistently look for ways to improve.

But before you start preparing for your first group session, you need to know the problem areas that will most likely weaken the effectiveness of your study group. Commit now to have the best Bible study group that you can possibly have. Ask the Lord to motivate you as a group leader and to steer you away from bad habits.

How to Guarantee a Poor Discussion Group:

1. Prepare inadequately.
2. Show improper attitude toward people in the group (lack of acceptance).
3. Fail to create an atmosphere of freedom and ease.
4. Allow the discussion to wander aimlessly.
5. Dominate the discussion yourself.
6. Let a small minority dominate the discussion.
7. Leave the discussion "in the air," so to speak, without presenting any concluding statements or some type of closure.
8. Ask too many "telling" or "trying" questions. (Don't ask individuals in your group pointed or threatening questions that might bring embarrassment to them or make them feel uncomfortable.)
9. End the discussion without adequate application points.
10. Do the same thing every time.
11. Become resentful and angry when people disagree with you. After all, you did prepare. You are the leader!
12. End the discussion with an argument.
13. Never spend any time with the members of your group other than the designated discussion meeting time.

Helpful Hints

One of the best ways to learn to be an effective Bible discussion leader is to sit under a good model. If you have had the chance to be in a group with an effective facilitator, think about the things that made him or her effective. Though you can learn much and shape many convictions from those good models, you can also glean some valuable lessons on what not to do from those who didn't do such a good job. Bill Donahue has done a good job of categorizing the leader's role in facilitating dynamic discussion into four key actions. They are easy to remember as he links them to the acrostic ACTS:

*A leader ACTS to facilitate discussions by:

Acknowledging everyone who speaks during a discussion.
Clarifying what is being said and felt.
Taking it to the group as a means of generating discussion.
Summarizing what has been said.

*Taken from *Leading Life-Changing Small Groups* ©1996 by the Willow Creek Association. Used by permission of Zondervan Publishing House.

Make a point to give each group member ample opportunity to speak. Pay close attention to any nonverbal communication (i.e. facial expressions, body language, etc.) that group members may use, showing their desire to speak. The four actions in Bill Donahue's acrostic will guarantee to increase your effectiveness, which will translate into your group getting more out of the Bible study. After all, isn't that your biggest goal?

Dealing with Talkative Timothy

Throughout your experiences of leading small Bible study groups, you will learn that there will be several stereotypes who will follow you wherever you go. One of them is **"Talkative Timothy."** He will show up in virtually every small group you will ever lead. (Sometimes this stereotype group member shows up as "Talkative Tammy.") "Talkative Timothy" talks too much, dominates the discussion time, and gives less opportunity for others to share. What do you do with a group member who talks too much? Below you will find some helpful ideas on managing the "Talkative Timothy's" in your group.

The best defense is a good offense. To deal with "Talkative Timothy" before he becomes a problem, one thing you can do is establish as a ground rule that no one can talk twice until everyone who wants to talk has spoken at least once. Another important ground rule is "no interrupting." Still another solution is to go systematically around the group, directing questions to people by name. When all else fails, you can resort to a very practical approach of sitting beside "Talkative Timothy." When you make it harder for him (or her) to make eye contact with you, you will create less chances for him to talk.

After taking one or more of these combative measures, you may find that "Timothy" is still a problem. You may need to meet with him (or her) privately. Assure him that you value his input, but remind him that you want to hear the comments of others as well. One way to diplomatically approach "Timothy" is to privately ask him to help you draw the less talkative members into the discussion. Approaching "Timothy" in this fashion may turn your dilemma into an asset. Most importantly, remember to love "Talkative Timothy."

Silent Sally

Another person who inevitably shows up is **"Silent Sally."** She doesn't readily speak up. Sometimes her silence is because she doesn't yet feel comfortable enough with the group to share her thoughts. Sometimes it is simply because she fears being rejected. Often her silence is because she is too polite to interrupt and thus is headed off at the pass each time she wants to speak by more aggressive (and less sensitive) members of the group. It is not uncommon in a mixed group to find that "Silent Sally" is married to "Talkative Timothy." (Seriously!) Don't mistakenly interpret her silence as meaning that she has nothing to contribute. Often those who are slowest to speak will offer the most meaningful contributions to the group. You can help "Silent Sally" make those significant contributions. Below are some ideas.

Make sure, first of all, that you are creating an environment that makes people comfortable. In a tactful way, direct specific questions to the less talkative in the group. Be careful though, not to put them on the spot with the more difficult or controversial questions. Become their biggest fan—make sure you cheer them on when they do share. Give them a healthy dose of affirmation. Compliment them afterward for any insightful contributions they make. You may want to sit across from them in the group so that it is easier to notice any non-verbal cues they give you when they want to speak. You should also come to their defense if another group member responds to them in a negative, stifling way. As you pray for each group member, ask that the Lord would help the quiet ones in your group to feel more at ease during the discussion time. Most of all, love "Silent Sally," and accept her as she is—even when she is silent!

Tangent Tom

We have already looked at "Talkative Timothy" and "Silent Sally." Now let's look at another of those stereotypes who always show up. Let's call this person, **"Tangent Tom."** He is the kind of guy who loves to talk even when he has nothing to say. "Tangent Tom" loves to chase rabbits regardless of where they go. When he gets the floor, you never know where the discussion will lead. You need to understand that not all tangents are bad, for sometimes much can be gained from discussion that is a little "off the beaten path." But diversions must be balanced against the purpose of the group. What is fruitful for one member may be fruitless for everyone else. Below are some ideas to help you deal with "Tangent Tom."

Evaluating Tangents

Ask yourself, "How will this tangent affect my group's chances of finishing the lesson?" Another way to measure the value of a tangent is by asking, "Is this something that will benefit all or most of the group?" You also need to determine whether there is a practical, spiritual benefit to this tangent. Paul advised Timothy to refuse foolish and ignorant speculations, knowing that they produce quarrels. (See 2 Timothy 2:23.)

Addressing Tangents:

1) Keep pace of your time, and use the time factor as your ally when addressing "Tangent Tom." Tactfully respond, "That is an interesting subject, but since our lesson is on _____, we'd better get back to our lesson if we are going to finish."

2) If the tangent is beneficial to one but fruitless to the rest of the group, offer to address that subject after class.

3) If the tangent is something that will benefit the group, you may want to say, "I'd like to talk about that more. Let's come back to that topic at the end of today's discussion, if we have time."

4) Be sure you understand what "Tangent Tom" is trying to say. It may be that he has a good and valid point, but has trouble expressing it or needs help in being more direct. Be careful not to quench someone whose heart is right, even if his methods aren't perfect. (See Proverbs 18:23.)

5) One suggestion for diffusing a strife-producing tangent is to point an imaginary shotgun at a spot outside the group and act like you are firing a shot. Then say, "That rabbit is dead. Now, where were we?"

6) If it is a continual problem, you may need to address it with this person privately.

7) Most of all, be patient with "Tangent Tom." God will use him in the group in ways that will surprise you!

Know–It–All Ned

The Scriptures are full of characters who struggled with the problem of pride. Unfortunately, pride isn't a problem reserved for the history books. It shows up today just as it did in the days the Scriptures were written. Pride is sometimes the root-problem of a know-it-all group member. **"Know-It-All Ned"** may have shown up in your group by this point. He may be an intellectual giant, or only a legend in his own mind. He can be very prideful and argumentative. "Ned" often wants his point chosen as the choice point, and he may be intolerant of any opposing views—sometimes to the point of making his displeasure known in very inappropriate ways. A discussion point tainted with the stench of pride is uninviting—no matter how well spoken! No one else in the group will want anything to do with this kind of attitude. How do you manage the "Know-It-All Ned's" who show up from time to time?

Evaluation

To deal with "Know-It-All Ned," you need to understand him. Sometimes the same type of action can be rooted in very different causes. You must ask yourself, "Why does 'Ned' come across as a know-it-all?" It may be that "Ned" has a vast reservoir of knowledge but hasn't matured in how he communicates it. Or perhaps "Ned" really doesn't know it all, but he tries to come across that way to hide his insecurities and feelings of inadequacy. Quite possibly, "Ned" is prideful and arrogant, and knows little of the Lord's ways in spite of the information and facts he has accumulated. Still another possibility is that Ned is a good man with a good heart who has a blind spot in the area of pride.

Application

"Know-It-All Ned" may be the most difficult person to deal with in your group, but God will use him in ways that will surprise you. Often it is the "Ned's" of the church that teach each of us what it means to love the unlovely in Gods strength, not our own. In 1 Thessalonians 5:14, the apostle Paul states, *"And we urge you, brethren, admonish the unruly, encourage the fainthearted, help the weak, be patient with all men."* In dealing with the "Ned's" you come across, start by assuming they are weak and need help until they give you reason to believe otherwise. Don't embarrass them by confronting them in public. Go to them in private if need be. Speak the truth in love. You may need to remind them of 1 Corinthians 13, that if we have all knowledge, but have not love, we are just making noise. First Corinthians is also where we are told, *"knowledge makes arrogant, but love edifies"* (8:1). Obviously there were some "Ned's" in the church at Corinth. If you sense that "Ned" is not weak or faint-hearted, but in fact is unruly, you will need to admonish him. Make sure you do so in private, but make sure you do it all the same. Proverbs 27:56 tells us, *"Better is open rebuke than love that is concealed. Faithful are the wounds of a friend, but deceitful are the kisses of an enemy."* Remember the last statement in 1 Thessalonians 5:14, *"be patient with all men."*

Agenda Alice

The last person we would like to introduce to you who will probably show up sooner or later is one we like to call **"Agenda Alice."** All of us from time to time can be sidetracked by our own agenda. Often the very thing we are most passionate about can be the thing that distracts us from our highest passion: Christ. Agendas often are not unbiblical, but imbalanced. At their root is usually tunnel-vision mixed with a desire for control. The small group, since it allows everyone to contribute to the discussion, affords "Agenda Alice" a platform to promote what she thinks is most important. This doesn't mean that she is wrong to avoid driving at night because opossums are being killed, but she is wrong to expect everyone to have the exact same conviction and calling that she does in the gray areas of Scripture. If not managed properly, she will either sidetrack the group from its main study objective or create a hostile environment in the group if she fails to bring people to her way of thinking. "Agenda Alice" can often be recognized by introductory catch phrases such as "Yes, but . . ." and "Well, I think. . . ." She is often critical of the group process and may become vocally critical of you. Here are some ideas on dealing with this type of person:

1) **Reaffirm** the group covenant.

   At the formation of your group you should have taken time to define some ground rules for the group. Once is not enough to discuss these matters of group etiquette. Periodically remind everyone of their mutual commitment to one another.

2) **Remember** that the best defense is a good offense.

   Don't wait until it is a problem to address a mutual vision for how the group will function.

3) **Refocus** on the task at hand.

   The clearer you explain the objective of each session, the easier it is to stick to that objective and the harder you make it for people to redirect attention toward their own agenda. Enlist the whole group in bringing the discussion back to the topic at hand. Ask questions like, "What do the rest of you think about this passage?"

4) **Remind** the group, "Remember, this week's lesson is about _____."

5) **Reprove** those who are disruptive.

   Confront the person in private to see if you can reach an understanding. Suggest another arena for the issue to be addressed such as an optional meeting for those in the group who would like to discuss the issue.

Remember the words of St. Augustine: "In essentials unity, in non-essentials liberty, in all things charity."

Adding Spice and Creativity

One of the issues you will eventually have to combat in any group Bible study is the enemy of boredom. This enemy raises its ugly head from time to time, but it shouldn't. It is wrong to bore people with the Word of God! Often boredom results when leaders allow their processes to become too predictable. As small group leaders, we tend to do the same thing in the same way every single time. Yet God the Creator, who spoke everything into existence is infinitely creative! Think about it. He is the one who not only created animals in different shapes and sizes, but different colors as well. When He created food, He didn't make it all taste or feel the same. This God of creativity lives in us. We can trust Him to give us creative ideas that will keep our group times from becoming tired and mundane. Here are some ideas:

When you think of what you can change in your Bible study, think of the five senses: (sight, sound, smell, taste, and feel).

SIGHT:
One idea would be to have a theme night with decorations. Perhaps you know someone with dramatic instincts who could dress up in costume and deliver a message from the person you are studying that week. Draw some cartoons on a marker board or handout.

SOUND:
Play some background music before your group begins. Sing a hymn together that relates to the lesson. If you know of a song that really hits the main point of the lesson, play it at the beginning or end.

SMELL:

This may be the hardest sense to involve in your Bible study, but if you think of a creative way to incorporate this sense into the lesson, you can rest assured it will be memorable for your group.

TASTE:

Some lessons will have issues that can be related to taste (e.g. unleavened bread for the Passover, etc.). What about making things less formal by having snacks while you study? Have refreshments around a theme such as "Chili Night" or "Favorite Fruits."

FEEL:

Any way you can incorporate the sense of feel into a lesson will certainly make the content more invigorating. If weather permits, add variety by moving your group outside. Whatever you do, be sure that you don't allow your Bible study to become boring!

Handling an Obviously Wrong Comment

From time to time, each of us can say stupid things. Some of us, however, are better at it than others. The apostle Peter had his share of embarrassing moments. One minute, he was on the pinnacle of success, saying, *"Thou art the Christ, the Son of the Living God"* (Matthew 16:16), and the next minute, he was putting his foot in his mouth, trying to talk Jesus out of going to the cross. Proverbs 10:19 states, *"When there are many words, transgression is unavoidable. . . ."* What do you do when someone in the group says something that is obviously wrong? First of all, remember that how you deal with a situation like this not only affects the present, but the future. Here are some ideas:

1) Let the whole group tackle it and play referee/peacemaker. Say something like, "That is an interesting thought, what do the rest of you think?"

2) Empathize. ("I've thought that before too, but the Bible says. . . .")

3) Clarify to see if what they said is what they meant. ("What I think you are saying is. . . .")

4) Ask the question again, focusing on what the Bible passage actually says.

5) Give credit for the part of the answer that is right and affirm that before dealing with what is wrong.

6) If it is a non-essential, disagree agreeably. ("I respect your opinion, but I see it differently.")
   Let it go —some things aren't important enough to make a big deal about them.

7) Love and affirm the person, even if you reject the answer.

Transitioning to the Next Study

For those of you who have completed leading a **Following God** Group Bible Study, congratulations! You have successfully navigated the waters of small group discussion. You have utilized one of the most effective tools of ministry—one that was so much a priority with Jesus, He spent most of His time there with His small group of twelve. Hopefully yours has been a very positive and rewarding experience. At this stage you may be looking forward to a break. It is not too early however, to be thinking and planning for what you will do next. Hopefully you have seen God use this study and this process for growth in the lives of those who have participated with you. As God has worked in the group, members should be motivated to ask the question, "What next?" As they do, you need to be prepared to give an answer. Realize that you have built a certain amount of momentum with your present study that will make it easier to do another. You want to take advantage of that momentum. The following suggestions may be helpful as you transition your people toward further study of God's Word.

❑ Challenge your group members to share with others what they have learned, and to encourage them to participate next time.

❑ If what to study is a group choice rather than a church-wide or ministry-wide decision made by others, you will want to allow some time for input from the group members in deciding what to do next. The more they have ownership of the study, the more they will commit to it.

❑ It is important to have some kind of a break so that everyone doesn't become study weary. At our church, we always look for natural times to start and end a study. We take the summer off as well as Christmas, and we have found that having a break brings people back with renewed vigor. Even if you don't take a break from meeting, you might take a breather from homework—or even get together just for fellowship.

❑ If you are able to end this study knowing what you will study next, some of your group members may want to get a head start on the next study. Be prepared to put books in their hands early.

❑ Make sure you end your study with a vision for more. Take some time to remind your group of the importance of the Word of God. As D. L. Moody used to say, "The only way to keep a broken vessel full is to keep the faucet running."

Evaluation
Becoming a Better Discussion Leader

The questions listed below are tools to assist you in assessing your discussion group. From time to time in the Leader's Guide, you will be advised to read through this list of evaluation questions in order to help you decide what areas need improvement in your role as group leader. Each time you read through this list, something different may catch your attention, giving you tips on how to become the best group leader that you can possibly be.

Read through these questions with an open mind, asking the Lord to prick your heart with anything specific He would want you to apply.

1. Are the group discussion sessions beginning and ending on time?

2. Am I allowing the freedom of the Holy Spirit as I lead the group in the discussion?

3. Do I hold the group accountable for doing their homework?

4. Do we always begin our sessions with prayer?

5. Is the room arranged properly (seating in a circle or semicircle, proper ventilation, adequate teaching aids)?

6. Is each individual allowed equal opportunity in the discussion?

7. Do I successfully bridle the talkative ones?

8. Am I successfully encouraging the hesitant ones to participate in the discussion?

9. Do I redirect comments and questions to involve more people in the interaction, or do I always dominate the discussion?

10. Are the discussions flowing naturally, or do they take too many "side roads" (diversions)?

11. Do I show acceptance to those who convey ideas with which I do not agree?

12. Are my questions specific, brief and clear?

13. Do my questions provoke thought, or do they only require pat answers?

14. Does each group member feel free to contribute or question, or is there a threatening or unnecessarily tense atmosphere?

15. Am I allowing time for silence and thought without making everyone feel uneasy?

16. Am I allowing the group to correct any obviously wrong conclusions that are made by others, or by myself (either intentionally to capture the group's attention or unintentionally)?

17. Do I stifle thought and discussion by assigning a question to someone before the subject of that question has even been discussed? (It will often be productive to assign a question to a specific person, but if you call on one person before you throw out a question, everyone else takes a mental vacation!)

18. Do I summarize when brevity is of the essence?

19. Can I refrain from expressing an opinion or comment that someone else in the group could just as adequately express?

20. Do I occasionally vary in my methods of conducting the discussion?

21. Am I keeping the group properly motivated?

22. Am I occasionally rotating the leadership to help others develop leadership?

23. Am I leading the group to specifically apply the truths that are learned?

24. Do I follow through by asking the group how they have applied the truths that they have learned from previous lessons?

25. Am I praying for each group member?

26. Is there a growing openness and honesty among my group members?

27. Are the group study sessions enriching the lives of my group members?

28. Have I been adequately prepared?

29. How may I be better prepared for the next lesson's group discussion?

30. Do I reach the objective set for each discussion? If not, why not? What can I do to improve?

31. Am I allowing the discussion to bog down on one point at the expense of the rest of the lesson?

32. Are the members of the group individually reaching the conclusions that I want them to reach without my having to give them the conclusions?

33. Do I encourage the group members to share what they have learned?

34. Do I encourage them to share the applications they have discovered?

35. Do I whet their appetites for next week's lesson discussion?

Getting Started
The First Meeting of Your Bible Study Group

Main Objectives of the first meeting: The first meeting is devoted to establishing your group and setting the course that you will follow through the study. Your primary goals for this session should be to . . .

❑ Establish a sense of group identity by starting to get to know one another.

❑ Define some ground rules to help make the group time as effective as possible.

❑ Get the study materials into the hands of your group members.

❑ Create a sense of excitement and motivation for the study.

❑ Give assignments for next week.

BEFORE THE SESSION

You will be most comfortable in leading this introductory session if you are prepared as much as possible for what to expect. This means becoming familiar with the place you will meet, and the content you will cover, as well as understanding any time constraints you will have.

Location—Be sure that you not only know how to find the place where you will be meeting, but also have time to examine the setup and make any adjustments to the physical arrangements. You never get a second chance to make a first impression.

Curriculum—You will want to get a copy of the study in advance of the introductory session, and it will be helpful if you do the homework for Lesson One ahead of time. This will make it easier for you to be able to explain the layout of the homework. It will also give you a contagious enthusiasm for what your group will be studying in the coming week. You will want to have enough books on hand for the number of people you expect so that they can get started right away with the study. You may be able to make arrangements with your church or local Christian Bookstore to bring copies on consignment. We would encourage you not to buy books for your members. Years of small group experience have taught that people take a study far more seriously when they make an investment in it.

Time—The type of group you are leading will determine the time format for your study. If you are doing this study for a Sunday school class or church study course, the time constraints may already be prescribed for you. In any case, ideally you will want to allow forty-five minutes to an hour for discussion.

WHAT TO EXPECT

When you embark on the journey of leading a small group Bible study, you are stepping into the stream of the work of God. You are joining in the process of helping others move toward spiritual maturity. As a small group leader, you are positioned to be a real catalyst in the lives of your group members, helping them to grow in their relationships with God. But you must remember, first and foremost, that whenever you step up to leadership in the kingdom of God, you are stepping down to serve. Jesus made it clear that leadership in the kingdom is not like leadership in the world. In Matthew 20:25, Jesus said, *"You know that the rulers of the Gentiles lord it over them, and their great men exercise authority over them."* That is the world's way to lead. But in Matthew 20:26–27, He continues, *"It is not so among you, but whoever wishes to become great among you shall be your servant, and whoever wishes to be first among you shall be your slave."* Your job as a small group leader is not to teach the group everything you have learned, but rather, to help them learn for themselves and from each other. It is a servant's role.

If you truly are to minister to the members of your group, you must start with understanding where they are, and join that with a vision of where you want to take them. In this introductory session, your group members will be experiencing several different emotions. They will be wondering, "Who is in my group?" and deciding "Do I like my group?" They will have a sense of excitement and anticipation, but also a sense of awkwardness as they try to find their place in this group. You will want to make sure that from the very beginning your group is founded with a sense of caring and acceptance. This is crucial if your group members are to open up and share what they are learning.

DURING THE SESSION

⧗ OPENING: 5–10 MINUTES
GETTING TO KNOW ONE ANOTHER

Opening Prayer—Remember that if it took the inspiration of God for people to write Scripture, it will also take His illumination for us to understand it. Have one of your group members open your time together in prayer.

Introductions—Take time to allow the group members to introduce themselves. Along with having the group members share their names, one way to add some interest is to have them add some descriptive information such as where they live or work. Just for fun, you could have them name their favorite breakfast cereal, most (or least) favorite vegetable, favorite cartoon character, their favorite city or country other than their own, etc.

Icebreaker—Take five or ten minutes to get the people comfortable in talking with each other. Since in many cases your small group will just now be getting to know one another, it will be helpful if you take some time to break the ice with some fun, non-threatening discussion. Below you will find a list of ideas for good icebreaker questions to get people talking.

____ What is the biggest risk you have ever taken?

____ If money were no object, where would you most like to take a vacation and why?

____ What is your favorite way to waste time?

____ If you weren't in the career you now have, what would have been your second choice for a career?

____ If you could have lived in any other time, in what era or century would you have chosen to live (besides the expected spiritual answer of the time of Jesus)?

____ If you became blind right now, what would you miss seeing the most?

____ Who is the most famous person you've known or met?

____ What do you miss most about being a kid?

____ What teacher had the biggest impact on you in school (good or bad)?

____ Of the things money can buy, what would you most like to have?

____ What is your biggest fear?

____ If you could give one miracle to someone else, what would it be (and to whom)?

____ Tell about your first job.

____ Who is the best or worst boss you ever had?

____ Who was your hero growing up and why?

⧗ DEFINING THE GROUP: 5–10 MINUTES
SETTING SOME GROUND RULES

There are several ways you can lay the tracks on which your group can run. One is simply to hand out a list of suggested commitments the members should make to the group. Another would be to hand out 3x5 cards and have the members themselves write down two or three commitments they would like to see everyone live out. You could then compile these into the five top ones to share at the following meeting. A third option is to list three (or more) commitments you are making to the group and then ask that they make three commitments back to you in return.

Here are some ideas for the types of ground rules that make for a good small group:

Leader:

____ To always arrive prepared

____ To keep the group on track so you make the most of the group's time

_____ To not dominate the discussion by simply teaching the lesson

_____ To pray for the group members

_____ To not belittle or embarrass anyone's answers

_____ To bring each session to closure and end on time

Member:

_____ To do my homework

_____ To arrive on time

_____ To participate in the discussion

_____ To not cut others off as they share

_____ To respect the different views of other members

_____ To not dominate the discussion

It is possible that your group may not need to formalize a group covenant, but you should not be afraid to expect a commitment from your group members. They will all benefit from defining the group up front.

⧗ INTRODUCTION TO THE STUDY: 15–20 MINUTES

As you introduce the study to the group members, your goal is to begin to create a sense of excitement about the Bible characters and applications that will be discussed. The most important question for you to answer in this session is "Why should I study _____?" You need to be prepared to guide them to finding that answer. Take time to give a brief overview of each leson.

⧗ CLOSING: 5–10 MINUTES

❑ Give homework for next week. In addition to simply reminding the group members to do their homework, if time allows, you might give them 5–10 minutes to get started on their homework for the first lesson.

❑ Key components for closing out your time are **a)** to review anything of which you feel they should be reminded, and **b)** to close in prayer. If time allows, you may want to encourage several to pray.

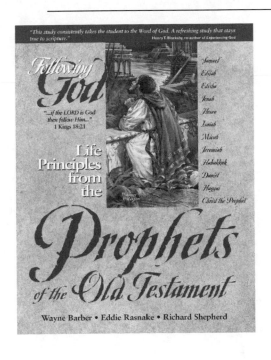

LIFE PRINCIPLES FROM THE PROPHETS OF THE OLD TESTAMENT

Samuel

MEMORY **I Samuel 12:24** VERSE

"Only fear the LORD and serve Him in truth with all your heart; for consider what great things He has done for you."

BEFORE THE SESSION

☐ Be sure to familiarize yourself with the chart on the life and ministry of Samuel at the end of Lesson 1.

☐ Spread your homework out rather than trying to cram everything into one afternoon or night. Perhaps use this as your daily quiet time.

☐ Always look for some personal applications which the Lord may have you share with the group. The more impact the Word makes in your heart the more enthusiasm you will communicate.

☐ As you study, write down any good discussion questions as they come to mind.

☐ **For additional study,** you can grasp the times in which Samuel lived and better prepare yourself towards leading the discussion by reading the book of Judges and/or Ruth. You may also want to look at some of the other **Following God** lessons centered around this period—**Gideon** and **Samson** in *Following God: Life Principles from the Old Testament*, **Ruth** and **Hannah** in *Following God: Life Principles from the Women of the Bible*, and **Saul** and **David** in *Following God: Life Principles from the Kings of the Old Testament*. The lessons in these **Following God**™ titles will help

you see the times and the ways of the people in Samuel's day.

☐ A good Bible dictionary article on "Samuel" will give you more background information. Dictionaries often help you see the historical setting in which the man or woman lived.

☐ Be transparent before the Lord and before your group. We are all learners—that's the meaning of the word "disciple."

WHAT TO EXPECT

Samuel was born because of the surrender of his mother, Hannah, to the Lord's will. This attitude of surrender became an indelible characteristic of Samuel's life. Samuel's attitude was not genetically inherited, but it became evident as he learned to walk with the Lord, hearing Him and obeying His Word. Samuel's life, as is the case in all our lives, was a process of growth, of knowing the Lord at deeper and deeper levels, of hearing and obeying by faith. Studying the life of Samuel can help us know the Lord at greater depths of faith when we listen to His Word. If we will listen with a teachable heart we will learn much more readily.

It is quite possible that many in your group will experience new insights or rich applications from their study this week. Some will realize how far they have strayed from the Word of God. Others will be affirmed in the steps of obedience they have taken. Expect the Lord to do a fresh work in you as well as in the members of your group. He waits to show Himself strong toward *those whose heart is fully His"* (see 1 Chronicles 16:9a). Some may have questions about the study or even about the validity of some portions of the Word of God. You can help them see the Bible as God's Word written in love. They can discover that this Book is eternal wisdom and is ever able to teach, reprove, correct, and train in righteousness (2 Timothy 3:16–17).

THE MAIN POINT

It is necessary to pay close attention to God's Word and obey Him promptly and fully.

DURING THE SESSION

⧗ OPENING: 5–10 MINUTES

Opening Prayer—You or one of your group members should open your time together in prayer.

Opening Illustration—A very dear missionary to China, Miss Bertha Smith, was part of the great Shantung Revival there in the 1930's. During her time in China, she faced the attack of the Japanese and was one of those expelled by the Communists in 1949. For years (until she died at the age of 100), she used countless opportunities to testify of the redemption found in Christ, the power of the Holy Spirit, and the sufficiency of the Word of God. Often when she gave her testimony, she would sing "How Firm a Foundation," a hymn she sang during the shelling of Yenchow by the Communists and also a hymn that she declared had seen her through three or four wars. The first verse declares:

> "How firm a foundation, ye saints of the Lord,
> Is laid for your faith in His excellent Word!
> What more can He say than to you He hath said,
> To you who for refuge to Jesus have fled?"

The members of your group can find that to be true for their lives as well. Ask God to solidify the faith of each one as you study the life of Samuel.

⧗ DISCUSSION: 30–40 MINUTES

Main Objective in Day One: The days in which Samuel was born were a time of spiritual decline when *"everyone did what was right in his own eyes"* (Judges 21:25). We want to see the heart and life of Hannah, Samuel's mother, and the life of Samuel (even as a young boy) against this backdrop. Below are some possible discussion questions for the Day One discussion. Check which questions you will use.

_____ What do you sense Samuel's home was like?

_____ How would you describe Hannah, Samuel's mother?

_____ What stands out about the spiritual atmosphere around the Tabernacle at Shiloh?

_____ How was Samuel different from Eli's sons?

Main Objective in Day Two: Just as the Word of God was the final word in Samuel's life, it is vital for us to make the Word central to all we think, say, and do. Check which discussion questions you will use for Day Two.

_____ Someone has well said, "You can choose your sin, but you cannot choose your consequences." How do you see that being worked out in the lives of Eli's sons?

_____ What does Samuel show us regarding how we are to respond to the Word of God?

_____ How would a fresh, clear understanding of the Word of God change the way things are in your home? At your job? In your community?

Main Objective in Day Three: The people of Israel had to learn that **knowing** the Word of God meant they were accountable to follow the will of the Lord as a nation and as individuals. Day Three focuses on surrender to the will of the Lord. Check which discussion questions for Day Three you might use.

_____ Israel did not have an in-depth knowledge of the Word of God. They treated the Ark of the Covenant in a somewhat superstitious way, almost like a "good-luck" charm. In what ways do we act like that in our Christian lives?

_____ Why do you think 1 Samuel 3:1 indicates that the *"word from the Lord was rare in those days"*?

_____ What are some "idols" that we must deal with? How do they distract us from hearing and seeing God and His will for our daily lives?

Main Objective in Day Four: Just as important as finding God's will is **doing** His will **in His way.** In Day Four, we see that Samuel learned this lesson when God made His choice for king of Israel. We must learn this lesson too. Some good discussion questions from Day Four might be . . .

_____ What have you learned from Samuel's life about dealing with sin (from both good or bad examples)?

_____ As Samuel grew older, he still had some things to learn about the Lord's ways. How does that relate to us?

_____ Like Samuel, we live in an era of spiritual decline. What does Samuel's life and ministry say to us today?

Day Five—Key Points in Application: The most significant application point from the life of Samuel is the importance of following the Word of the Lord with a humble, teachable heart. Choose one or two discussion questions from the list below.

_____ Samuel was **available** to the plan of God. Being available means being surrendered to do His will His way—when He says, how He says. Do you ever struggle with "I'm not available for that" attitudes? As leaders, you may want to share some struggles you have had.

_____ Samuel was also **teachable.** What do you think gets in the way of us being teachable?

_____ What are some ways you are honoring the Word of God as your source of wisdom and direction?

_____ What do you think of people who treat the Scriptures as just another book of good opinions, another option on the shelf of options?

⏳ CLOSING: 5–10 MINUTES

❏ **Summarize**—Restate the key points highlighted in the class. Take a few moments to preview next week's lesson, **"Elijah: Following God When Those Around You Do Not."**

❏ **Encourage** the group to do their homework.

❏ **Pray**—Close in prayer.

⚒ TOOLS FOR GOOD DISCUSSION ⚒

Some who are reading this have led small-group Bible studies many times. Here is an important word of warning: experience alone does not make you a more effective discussion leader. In fact, experience can make you **less effective.** You see, the more experience you have the more comfortable you will be at the task. Unfortunately, for some that means becoming increasingly comfortable in doing a bad job. Taking satisfaction with mediocrity translates into taking the task less seriously. It is easy to wrongly assert that just because one is experienced, he or she can successfully "shoot from the hip," so to speak. If you really want your members to get the most out of this study, you need to be dissatisfied with simply doing an adequate job and make it your aim to do an excellent job. A key to excellence is to regularly evaluate yourself to see that you are still doing all that you want to be doing. We have prepared a list of over thirty evaluation questions for you to review from time to time. The list of questions can be found on page 11 in this Leader's Guide. The examination questions will help to jog your memory and, hopefully, will become an effective aid in improving the quality of your group discussion. Review the evaluation questions list, and jot down below two or three action points for you to begin implementing next week.

ACTION POINTS:

1. _____

_____

2. _____

_____

3. _____

_____

Elijah

MEMORY **Colossians 4:17** VERSE

"Take heed to the ministry which you have received in the Lord, that you may fulfill it

BEFORE THE SESSION

❑ An important historical note is that Elijah ministered after the division of Israel into two kingdoms—the conservative Southern Kingdom (Judah), ruled over by the descendents of David, and the liberal Northern Kingdom (still called Israel), ruled by whoever could seize power. Elijah was a prophet to that Northern Kingdom.

❑ Remember that your goal is not to teach the lesson, but to facilitate discussion. Think of open-ended questions that will generate dialogue.

❑ For an enhanced understanding of the times in which Elijah ministered, see *Following God: Life Principles from the Kings of the Old Testament*, Lesson 6, on **"King Ahab: The Sins of Serving Self."** This wicked king reigned in Israel during the ministry of the prophet Elijah.

❑ Make sure your own heart is right with God. Be willing to be transparent with the group about your own life experiences and mistakes. This will make it easier for them to open up.

❑ Don't be afraid of chasing tangents for a while if they capture the interest of the group as a whole, but don't sacrifice the rest of the group to belabor the questions of one member. Trust God to lead you.

WHAT TO EXPECT

The danger of dealing with a character as familiar as Elijah is that, although most everyone will have some knowledge of certain events in his life, few will have seriously studied him. What they know of Elijah is woven from the snippets they have heard of him in sermons and the like. Make sure that, if nothing else, everyone goes away with some kind of grasp on the "received vs. achieved" principle. Many will find this principle to be an unfamiliar concept, but hopefully the concept will be a liberating one to them. God will be prompting many in your group to follow Elijah's example. They will need to be reminded that the keys are **a) walking** with God, and **b) waiting** on God. To experience "received" ministry and a "God-initiated" life, we have to be willing to be patient and let God have His way with us.

> **THE MAIN POINT**
> True ministry is "received, not achieved."
> Elijah models for us what it means to live a
> God-initiated life instead of a self-initiated,
> self-directed life.

DURING THE SESSION

⏳ OPENING: 5–10 MINUTES

Opening Prayer—Ask someone to open your time in prayer.

Opening Illustration—The great hymn, "Have Thine Own Way" was written in 1902 by Adelaide Pollard during a time she referred to as suffering "a great distress of soul." Shortly before, she had tried unsuccessfully to raise funds for a missionary trip to Africa. God met with her in a prayer meeting, and the result was these words to this powerful hymn:

> "Have Thine own way, Lord! Have Thine own way!
> Thou art the Potter; I am the clay.
> Mould me and make me after Thy will,
> While I am waiting, yielded and still."

She had learned that true ministry is **received**, not achieved.

⏳ DISCUSSION: 30–40 MINUTES

Once your group gets talking, you will find that all you need to do is keep the group directed and flowing with a question or two or a pointed observation. You are the gatekeeper of discussion. Don't be afraid to ask someone to elaborate further or to ask a quiet member of the group what they think of someone else's comments. Time will not allow you to discuss every single question in the lesson one at a time. Instead, make it your goal to cover the main ideas of each day and help the group to share what they learned personally. You don't have to use all the discussion questions. They are there for you to pick and choose from.

Main Objective in Day One: The main objective here is to see the central role in Elijah's life of *"the Word of the Lord."* This refers not just to the Scriptures, but specifically to his hearing from God and being directed by God as he walked in fellowship with Him. While we will not experience God audibly speaking to us on a day-to-day basis, we are going to experience His leading as we walk with Him. Check which discussion questions you will use.

_____ What do you think the text means by the phrase, *"the word of the Lord"*?

_____ How was Elijah's hearing from God different than what we experience today?

_____ How was it the same?

_____ A companion idea here is that "where God guides, He provides." How do we see that in Elijah's experience?

_____ What things get in the way of us hearing from God?

Main Objective in Day Two: Here we see that the miracle on Mt. Carmel was not a matter of Elijah coming up with a good idea and asking God to bless it, but rather doing all, Elijah says, *"at thy word"* (1 Kings 18:36).

_____ From where does the idea come for Elijah's challenge?

_____ What do you think God is trying to show Israel through His dealings here at Mt. Carmel? Why?

_____ James says Elijah's prayer is an example of "effective prayer." What do you learn about prayer from his example?

_____ Does prayer have to be long to be effective?

_____ What keeps our prayers from being effective?

Main Objective in Day Three: Day Three introduces us to some of Elijah's humanness. There is always the danger of placing the people God uses on such a pedestal that we lose our ability to relate with them. Not only does Elijah show us that the Christian life is going to have its share of "highs" and "lows," but through him we also see that the highs are often followed by lows. Examine the discussion questions below, and determine which questions you might want to use in your discussion for Day Three.

_____ How is this experience of Elijah different than what we saw on Mt. Carmel?

_____ Why do you think Elijah struggled with trusting God with the threat on his life?

_____ What is the good news in how God dealt with Elijah's suicidal prayer?

_____ What conclusions can we draw from Elijah's experience concerning how we manage our own spiritual highs and lows?

Main Objective in Day Four: In Day Four we see the potential pitfall into which each of us can stumble: that is, thinking we are the only one standing for God. Like Elijah, we can convince ourselves that God needs us and wrongly assume that without us His purposes cannot be realized. Check which discussion questions you will use from Day Four.

_____ What is wrong with Elijah's perspective here?

_____ Have you ever felt that you were the only one standing for God?

_____ What does Elijah's experience say to you about loneliness?

_____ Did anything else stand out to you from Day Four?

Day Five—Key Points in Application: The most important application point from Elijah's life is that he followed God's initiation and direction most of the time. When he followed God, he was able to see God do more for him than anything he could do for God. Check which discussion questions you will use for Day Five.

_____ Can you see any examples in your own life or those around you of ministry that is **achieved** (man-initiated) instead of **received** (initiated by God)?

_____ Did God show you anything through this lesson you need to do differently?

⧖ CLOSING: 5–10 MINUTES

❑ **Summarize**—restate the key points that were highlighted in the class.

❑ **Remind** your group that the Christian life is not about trying hard to be like Jesus, but it is about totally surrendering our lives to God and letting Him work through us.

❑ **Preview**—Take a few moments to preview next week's lesson on **"Elisha: Putting Down the Idols in our Lives."** Encourage the group to be sure to do their homework.

❑ **Pray**—Close in prayer.

TOOLS FOR GOOD DISCUSSION

Bill Donahue, in his book, _Leading Life-Changing Small Groups_ (Grand Rapids: Zondervan Publishing House, 1996), lists four facilitator actions that will produce dynamic discussion. These four actions are easy to remember because they are linked through the acrostic method to the word, **ACTS.** You will profit from taking time to review this information in the "Helpful Hints" section of **How to Lead a Small Group Bible Study,** which is on page 5 of this Leader's Guide book.

Elisha

MEMORY **I John 5:21** VERSE

"Little children, guard yourselves from idols."

BEFORE THE SESSION

❑ Pray each day for the members of your group—that they spend time in the Word, grasp the message God wants to bring to their lives, and that they surrender to what God is saying.

❑ Do your homework—don't procrastinate!

❑ Remember, Elijah (last week's lesson) was mentor to Elisha. Keep that connection in view.

❑ Mark those ideas and questions you want to discuss as you go through the study. Those, along with the questions listed below, can personalize the discussion to fit your group. Think of the needs of your group and be looking for applicable questions and discussion starters.

❑ To better understand the times and the depths of Israel's idolatry, see *Following God: Life Principles from the Kings of the Old Testament,* Lesson 6, entitled **"Ahab: The Sins of Serving Self"** as well as Lesson 7 on **"Jehoshaphat: Unequally Yoked."**

❑ Ever remain teachable. Look first for what God is saying to you.

❑ Prepare yourself to be transparent and open about what God is teaching you. Nothing is quite as contagious as the joy of discovering new treasures in the Word.

WHAT TO EXPECT

For some in your group the dangers of idolatry are something reserved for some tribe on an island in the middle of the Pacific, not for modern society. However, we see in the life of Elisha just how close idols can be—as close as the breath we breathe. This can be an eye-opening and heart-revealing truth. Take this opportunity to sharpen your group's awareness of the idols of today, and then help them see the subtlety of idolatry. Elisha can be a true friend to help lead them out of the pit of idolatry and onto the solid ground of a surrendered walk with the true and living God.

THE MAIN POINT
We are to faithfully follow the true and living God and ever guard ourselves against idolatry in any form.

DURING THE SESSION

⧖ **OPENING: 5 MINUTES**

Opening Prayer—Remember that the Lord is the Teacher, and He wants us to depend on Him as we open the Scriptures.

Opening Illustration—In one of His acts of judgment on faithless Israel in the wilderness, God sent poisonous serpents among the people. In Numbers 21, we read the story of God directing Moses to make a bronze serpent and lift it on a pole. All who had been bitten by these snakes need only look at the pole and be healed. The bronze serpent pole is an Old Testament picture of Christ (John 3:14). Yet in King Hezekiah's day, we learn that it had to be destroyed. It had become an idol to the people (2 Kings 18:4). They named it *"Nehushtan"* and burned incense to it. The human heart is able to take things that should point us to God and turn them into objects of worship. Whether it is creation or our blessings or even the past working of God, there is ever the danger of placing something ahead of God in our hearts. That is the danger we see Elisha confronting.

⏳ DISCUSSION: 30–40 MINUTES

Keep the group directed along the main highway of Elisha. You may have a pointed observation that helps sharpen the focus of the group. Encourage some to elaborate further on a key point, or ask a quiet member of the group what he or she thinks of someone's comments. Watch the time, knowing that you cannot cover every single question in the lesson. Seek to cover the main ideas of each day and help the group to share what they learned personally.

Main Objective in Day One: You should desire that you and your group see the necessity of following the true God in the midst of any tests or challenges that you may face. Elisha faced certain tests concerning his willingness to follow Elijah. He learned to trust in God's ways and experienced God's power as Elijah had done. He also had to trust God that the people would listen to him as God's spokesman. Check which discussion questions you will use from Day One.

_____ What was Israel like in the days of Elijah and Elisha? What parallels do you see today?

_____ Elijah faced some struggles. How did the Lord deal with him and with his struggles? How did the Lord encourage Elijah?

_____ What do you think it meant for Elisha to leave behind his parents and the family business? Are you facing a similar challenge or call on your life?

_____ How did Elisha respond to the various tests he faced? What can we learn from Elisha's responses for the tests we face?

Main Objective in Day Two: Here we learn that the Lord is the **living** God, the true provider, who longs for His people to look to Him and to follow Him—not some **dead** idol. You want to make sure your group catches that one point. Check which discussion questions you will use for your discussion of Day Two.

_____ Why do you think many in Israel superstitiously followed Baal and Baal worship like the nations around them? How did Elisha show them the truth about the true God?

_____ What are some modern "gods/idols" today? How do we follow the "popular" gods of those around us? How can we show them the truth about the true God?

_____ Think of the many ways God used Elisha to reveal Himself as the **Living God** in today's Scriptures. Name or list those ways or write them on a marker board.

_____ How has God revealed Himself as the **Living God** today? Some in your group may want to share ways they have seen God alive in their lives and circumstances this week or in recent weeks.

Main Objective in Day Three: Day Three introduces us to the ways of God among "the nations." He is Lord of all the earth, not just Israel. Check a discussion question or two below that you find to be useful for your discussion about Day Three.

_____ How does God deal with those from other nations? What does God's dealings with Naaman tell you about the ways of God?

_____ How did Elisha deal with someone from another nation? What was his focus? In the New Testament, Peter declared *"I most certainly understand now that God is not one to show partiality"* or is *"no respecter of persons"* (Acts 10:34). Neither was Elisha partial. What does that say to you?

_____ What do you see about God's protective care for His people in the incident of the army surrounding Elisha? Ask different members of your group to give one of the purposes of the angels according to Hebrews 1:14.

_____ What is God's desire for the nations? You may want to read some additional Scriptures not found in this lesson, such as Joshua 4:19–24 (especially verse 24), 1 Kings 8:41–43, and Matthew 28:18–20.

Main Objective in Day Four: For Day Four, we want to emphasize the faithfulness of God. He is faithful to His people in every detail of their lives and is committed to seeing them walk with Him, following Him as their God. Therefore, He is committed to child-training and discipline. Check which discussion questions you will use from Day Four .

_____ What kind of discipline did God bring upon Israel through Hazael of Syria? What does this show us about God's faithfulness to His people?

_____ What role did Jehu play in God's dealings with Israel? What do you discover about the faithfulness and the ways of God in all Jehu did?

_____ What does 2 Kings 13:22–23 mean to you personally?

_____ Read Hebrews 12:1–13. How does that passage speak to you about the faithfulness of God in training and dealing with His children?

Day Five—Key Points in Application: The most important application point is found in the delight of walking with the true and living God, while always being aware of the ever-present danger of idolatry. Below, check the questions that you might consider using in your discussion.

_____ We need to be nourished on "sound" or "healthy" doctrine—the Word of God. How can you be sure to guard yourself from unhealthy teaching?

_____ Has this lesson brought to mind any worldly opinions that have gotten mixed in with what you know in Scripture? Share some of these.

_____ What about idolatry in **your** life? Remember when the apostle John was writing 1 John, he was talking to Christians ("*little children*") who knew the Scriptures. The dangers of idolatry are always near. That's why we must "guard" ourselves. Review some of the idols we may face in today's world.

_____ What can you do to increase your intake of the Word of God and intensify your watchfulness against idolatry?

⌛ CLOSING: 5–10 MINUTES

❑ **Summarize**—Restate the key points the group shared (Review the objectives for each of the days found at the beginning of these leader notes).

❑ **Remind**—Using the memory verse (1 John 5:21), remind the group that idols are still around today. We must stay on guard.

❑ **Preview**—Take time to preview next week's lesson, **"Jonah: Following God When You Don't Want To."**

❑ **Pray**—Close in prayer.

✂ TOOLS FOR GOOD DISCUSSION 🔨

One of the people who shows up in every group is a person we call **"Talkative Timothy."** Talkative Timothy tends to talk too much and dominates the discussion time by giving less opportunity for others to share. What do you do with a group member who talks too much? In the "Helpful Hints" section of **How to Lead a Small Group Bible Study** (p. 5), you'll find some practical ideas on managing the "Talkative Timothy's" in your group.

4

Jonah

MEMORY **I Samuel 15:22** VERSE

"Has the Lord as much delight in burnt offerings and sacrifices as in obeying the voice of the Lord? Behold, to obey is better than sacrifice, and to heed than the fat of rams."

BEFORE THE SESSION

❑ Be sure to do your own study far enough in advance so as not to be rushed. You want to allow God time to speak to you personally.

❑ Don't feel that you have to use all of the discussion questions listed below. You may have come up with others on your own, or you may find that time will not allow you to use them all. These questions are to serve you, not for you to serve.

❑ You are the gatekeeper of the discussion. Do not be afraid to "reel the group back in" if they get too far away from the lesson.

❑ Remember to keep a highlight pen ready as you study to mark any points you want to be sure to discuss.

WHAT TO EXPECT

The story of Jonah is the most human portrait of any of the prophets. It accurately records his rebellion against God's plan for him and shows how God dealt with him to bring him to a place of obedience. The account of Jonah and the great fish is so familiar that we run the risk of resembling that old adage, "familiarity breeds contempt." Yet, as you can see, there are some very practical lessons to be learned

from his life—the main one being that we cannot succeed in running from God. Because God is who He is, He is able to keep turning up the heat through the circumstances of our lives, until we yield to His will and way. An important point to acknowledge, however, is that even submitting to God's will can be done with a wrong heart. To do the right actions alone is not enough. God desires that our hearts become yielded to Him, not simply that we acquiesce to His will because we have to.

> ### THE MAIN POINT
> The main point to be seen here is God's grace in the midst of Jonah's very reluctant obedience.

DURING THE SESSION

⏳ **OPENING: 5–10 MINUTES**

Opening Prayer—Remember that if it took the inspiration of God for people to write Scripture, it will also take His illumination for us to understand it. Have one of the more serious minded members of your group open your time together in prayer.

Opening Illustration—A good hook for introducing this lesson might be the story of the little school boy who was made to sit in the corner during class as punishment for repeatedly standing when he should not. When the teacher came by and said, "Now, that is more like it," he replied in rebellion, "I may be sitting down on the outside, but I am standing up on the inside!" Such reluctant submission is not what the Lord desires. Yet that is what we see in Jonah.

⧖ DISCUSSION: 30–40 MINUTES

Here is a little tip to enhance the quality of your group's discussion. Don't be afraid to ask someone to elaborate further on their comments ("Explain what you mean, Barbara.") or to ask a quiet member of the group what he or she thinks of someone else's comments ("What do you think, Dave?"). Time will not allow you to discuss every single question in the lesson one at a time. Instead, make it your goal to cover the main ideas of each day, and help the group to share what they learned personally.

Main Objective in Day One: In Day One, the main objective is to reveal the downward spiral Jonah experiences when he runs from God's plan and purpose. Jonah was called to a purpose that he didn't like, so instead of obeying, he rebelled and ran from God. Every Christian has done the same thing at some point, so you should have no trouble getting your group members to identify with Jonah. Check which discussion questions from Day One you will use.

_____ Have someone restate the assignment God gave to Jonah in verses 1 and 2.

_____ Can you think of a purpose God has given to you at some time that you have struggled with?

_____ How did God deal with Jonah's rebellion?

_____ What do you think was going through Jonah's mind as he was running?

Main Objective in Day Two: In Day Two we learn the key principle, "If you don't get right when God sends the storm, you will get right when troubles grow far worse!" You'll want to make sure that your group understands that God is willing and able to turn up the heat if we are unwilling to submit to Him. Check the discussion questions below that might apply to your group.

_____ What was Jonah's response to the storm God sent his way?

_____ What are some of the storms God brings into our lives to get our attention?

_____ Why do you think it took Jonah so long to surrender to the Lord's call?

_____ We see that it wasn't until Jonah prayed that God commanded the fish to vomit him onto the land. What is the message for us in that?

_____ The last statement of Day Two says, "When God brings calamity upon us for our rebellion, He will not relent until we repent." Do you agree or disagree with that statement?

Main Objective in Day Three: Day Three introduces us to the results of Jonah's repentance. The fruit his preaching at Nineveh bore is the greatest evangelistic response recorded in Scripture—greater even than Peter's preaching at Pentecost. Jonah's repentance allowed him to be a part of a mighty moving of God. Check which discussion questions from Day Three you will use.

_____ What stands out to you from Jonah's message to Nineveh?

_____ Why do you think the people of Nineveh responded as they did?

_____ How does our preaching today differ from what you see here?

_____ Verse 10 tells us that when the people repented, God relented concerning the calamity. How does that apply to us?

_____ What do you think true repentance is?

Main Objective in Day Four: In Day Four we see more of Jonah's humanness. Sadly, though he was finally obedient to God's charge, he was disappointed that God did not judge the Ninevites anyway. Below, check any discussion questions from Day Four that may be appropriate for your group.

_____ What are some reasons we don't rejoice when God shows mercy to the guilty?

_____ What prejudices do you struggle with?

_____ We see that Jonah's reluctance was rooted in the fact that he did not agree with God's plan. Are there any areas in your life where you struggle with disagreeing with God's plan?

_____ Did you have any unanswered questions from this week's lesson?

Day Five—Key Points in Application: The most important application point from the life of Jonah is that God did not allow him to succeed in running away from His will. Check which discussion questions you will use from Day Five.

_____ Can you think of a time where you ran from God's will?

_____ Hebrews 12 indicates two wrong responses to God's disciplines: **a)** to regard it lightly, and **b)** to faint when we are reproved. What would these wrong responses look like in practical terms?

_____ What are some areas where you struggle with recognizing people *"…according to the flesh"*?

⌛ CLOSING: 5–10 MINUTES

❑ **Summarize**—Restate the key points that were highlighted in the class. You may also want to briefly review the main objectives for each of the days found in these leader notes.

❑ **Remind** your group that the victorious Christian life is not attained when we try hard to be like Jesus, but when we surrender our lives to God and let Him work through us.

❑ **Ask** your group what they think the key applications from Day Five are.

❑ **Preview**—Take a few moments to preview next week's lesson on **"Hosea: Returning to the Lord."** Encourage your group to do their homework.

❑ **Pray**—Close in prayer.

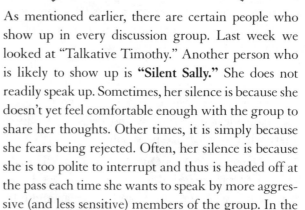 

TOOLS FOR GOOD DISCUSSION

As mentioned earlier, there are certain people who show up in every discussion group. Last week we looked at "Talkative Timothy." Another person who is likely to show up is **"Silent Sally."** She does not readily speak up. Sometimes, her silence is because she doesn't yet feel comfortable enough with the group to share her thoughts. Other times, it is simply because she fears being rejected. Often, her silence is because she is too polite to interrupt and thus is headed off at the pass each time she wants to speak by more aggressive (and less sensitive) members of the group. In the "Helpful Hints" section of **How to Lead a Small Group Bible Study** (p. 6), you'll find some practical ideas on managing the "Silent Sally's" in your group.

5

Hosea

MEMORY **2 Corinthians 11:2–3** VERSES

"I am jealous for you with a godly jealousy; for I betrothed you to one husband, that to Christ I might present you as a pure virgin. But I am afraid, lest as the serpent deceived Eve by his craftiness, your minds should be led astray from the simplicity and purity of devotion to Christ."

BEFORE THE SESSION

❏ Resist the temptation to do all your homework in one sitting or to put it off until the last minute. You will not be fully prepared if you study in this fashion.

❏ Make sure to mark down any discussion questions that come to mind as you study.

❏ If you want to do further study, look at 1 and 2 Kings and 1 and 2 Chronicles and read about the kings who ruled while Hosea ministered.

❏ Remember your need to trust God with your study. The Holy Spirit is always the best teacher, so stay sensitive to Him!

WHAT TO EXPECT

In this lesson, assume that all your group members need to better understand how to return to the Lord when they stray. They will all eventually need this for their own walk, and they will all, sooner or later, be in a position to help someone else who will need it. Don't worry so much about covering all the details of the study. Make sure that you devote adequate time to clearly explaining and answering any questions they have about returning to the Lord.

> ### THE MAIN POINT
> The main call of Hosea is to "return to the Lord," and the main point to be seen in this lesson is how we do that.

In order to understand Hosea's instruction, it is necessary to look at the day in which he lived and the sins of Israel that he confronted. His powerful showdown with the spiritual adultery of Israel was made more personal by the physical adultery of his own wife.

DURING THE SESSION

⌛ **OPENING: 5–10 MINUTES**

Opening Prayer—Remember to have one of your group members open your time together in prayer.

Opening Illustration—Winston Churchill, Prime Minister of Great Britain during World War II, not only was a great leader, but also earned a reputation as the "king of the verbal comeback." He seemed to be at his best while sparring with his main political adversary, Lady Astor. On one occasion, being quite put out with him, she uttered, "Sir Churchill, if I were your wife, I would put arsenic in your tea!" to which Churchill retorted, "Lady Astor, if I were your husband, I would drink it!" On another occasion at a party the two met in the elevator as they were leaving. Lady Astor remarked with contempt, "Sir Churchill, I perceive that you are drunk." The quick-witted Churchill returned, "Yes Lady Astor, and you are ugly," and then added, "and tomorrow I shall be sober!" No one, however, was armed with a greater comeback than the prophet Hosea. Every time someone would comment about his unfaithful, harlot wife, he could return, "And that is exactly what you are to God."

⏳ DISCUSSION: 30–40 MINUTES

By now, you should realize that your job is not to teach this lesson, but to facilitate discussion. Do your best to guide the group to the right answers, but don't be guilty of making a point **someone else** in the group could easily make.

Main Objective in Day One: In Day One, the main objective is to see how God worked His message into Hosea's life. Through his marriage to an unfaithful bride, he was able to feel the heart of God toward prodigal Israel. Check which questions you might use for your discussion on Day One.

_____ Why do you think God wanted Hosea to have a harlot for a wife?

_____ What struggles do you think Hosea had in ministry because of his wife?

_____ How is Gomer's harlotry a good parallel to Israel's wanderings from God?

_____ What do you think about Hosea's children?

_____ Were there any questions raised by your study?

Main Objective in Day Two: In Day Two, we learn some of the specifics of the sins in Israel God confronted through the prophet Hosea. Make sure that your group grasps the concept that Israel had committing "spiritual" adultery by their dalliance with other religions. Not mentioned in the workbook study, but something worth discussing, is that the words used in Hosea 2:2 are similar to those used in the Jewish formula for divorce. Check which discussion questions you will use from Day Two.

_____ What kinds of actions in Israel does God associate with "spiritual adultery"?

_____ What are some equivalents to "spiritual adultery" in our day?

_____ What correlation do you see between Israel's straying and their lack of gratitude for God's blessings?

_____ Israel's unfaithfulness to the Lord included the hypocrisy of rituals with no meaning in their hearts. What are some things that can become meaningless rituals to us today?

Main Objective in Day Three: Day Three introduces us to the heart of God through His message to "return to the Lord." It is a powerful reminder that at the heart of the Scriptures is God's willingness to accept us back when we stray. Every member of your group will be able to relate in some way with wandering from the Lord, and will benefit from Hosea's invitation. It is worth reminding the group that the word "return" appears 22 times in Hosea. Check the discussion questions for Day Three you that appeal to you.

_____ What stands out to you most about the way God draws His unfaithful spouse back in Chapter 2?

_____ What similarities do you see between Hosea and what God did with us through Christ?

_____ Hosea 2:6 indicates that God would _"hedge up her way with thorns."_ Have you ever experienced God doing that as you wandered?

_____ Have you ever experienced God "winning" your love back? How?

_____ Do you agree with the statement, "We don't 'find' God—He finds us"?

Main Objective in Day Four: In Day Four, we see how God woos His prodigal people back to Himself. Some key points you want your group members to catch are: **1)** confession is for our benefit, not just God's, **2)** repentance **always** accompanies true confession, and, most importantly, **3)** repentance will involve "plowing the fallow (unplowed) ground." Make sure they see that any area of our lives from which we exclude God will become hard, fallow ground. It takes a choice to allow the plow of His Word into those areas to break up the hardness. Check the questions for Day Four that you will use in your discussion on Hosea.

_____ Why do we need to confess sin if God already knows everything?

_____ Do you think it is possible to truly confess without repenting?

_____ Hosea 14:5–8 pictures the freshness of life after repentance. Have you ever experienced this repentance?

_____ How do you think "fallow" ground (hard, unplowed ground) develops in our lives?

_____ Name some examples of "fallow ground" that you have seen or experienced.

Day Five—Key Points in Application: The most important application out of Day Five is that we are all prodigals, and therefore we all need to know how to return to the Lord. Express to your group that the keys to repentance and returning to God are: **a)** remembering what it was like to walk with God, and **b)** making a choice to return. Check which discussion questions from Day Five you will use.

_____ What stands out to you about the parable of the prodigal son?

_____ What gets in our way of returning to the Lord?

_____ Have you ever tried to "return" to God, expecting God to place you on "probation"?

_____ Is there anything you still don't understand about returning to the Lord when you stray?

⧗ CLOSING: 5–10 MINUTES

❑ **Summarize**—Restate the key points.

❑ **Ask** your group what they consider to be the key applications for Day Five.

❑ **Sing**—If your meeting space allows, you may want to sing together the last verse of "Come Thou Fount of Every Blessing." Explain the relevance of this song to the Hosea study. (See p. 77 in *Following God: Life Principles from the Prophets of the Old Testament*.)

❑ **Pray**—Ask someone in your group to close your session with prayer.

TOOLS FOR GOOD DISCUSSION

Hopefully your group is functioning smoothly at this point, but perhaps you recognize the need for improvement. In either case, you will benefit from taking the time to evaluate yourself and your group. Without evaluation, you will judge your group on subjective emotions. You may think everything is fine and miss some opportunities to improve your effectiveness. You may be discouraged by problems you are confronting when you ought to be encouraged that you are doing the right things and making progress. A healthy Bible-study group is not one without problems, but is one that recognizes its problems and deals with them the right way. At this point in the course, as you and your group are nearly halfway completed with the study of the Old Testament prophets, it is important to examine yourself and see if there are any mid-course corrections that you feel are necessary to implement. Review the evaluation questions list found on page 11 of this Leader's Guide, and jot down two or three action points to begin implementing next week. Perhaps you have made steady improvements since the first time you answered the evaluation questions at the beginning of the course. If so, your improvements should challenge you to be an even better group leader for the final seven lessons in the study.

ACTION POINTS:

1. _____

_____

2. _____

_____

3. _____

_____

6

Isaiah

MEMORY **2 Timothy 2:21** VERSE

"Therefore, if a man cleanses himself from these things, he will be a vessel for honor, sanctified, useful to the Master, prepared for every good work."

BEFORE THE SESSION

❑ Remember the Boy Scout motto: **BE PREPARED!** The main reason a Bible study flounders is because the leader is unprepared and tries to "shoot from the hip," so to speak.

❑ Make sure to mark down any discussion questions that come to mind as you study.

❑ If you want to do further study, look at 1 and 2 Kings and 1 and 2 Chronicles, and read about the kings who ruled while Isaiah ministered. You may also benefit from doing the lesson on Hezekiah from *Following God: Life Principles from the Kings*. The revival during Hezekiah's reign was influenced by the ministry of Isaiah.

❑ Don't forget to pray for the members of your group and for your time of studying together. You don't want to be satisfied with what **you** can do. You want to see God do what only **He** can do!

WHAT TO EXPECT

In this lesson, realize that all of us, sooner or later, will fall prey to comparing ourselves to others around us instead of to the holy standards of God.

Make sure you allow time for members of your group to share honestly about their struggles. Realize that there may be some sin God wants to deal with so that He can make each member more useable to Him in His work. Be sensitive to any questions this lesson may surface about ministry, and guard your group from applying it only to those with a "vocational" ministry.

> ### THE MAIN POINT
> The main point to be seen in this lesson is that, before God can use us, He must first make us useable.

In other words, before He can do a work **through** us, He must first do a work **in** us. Before Isaiah *"saw the Lord"* his message was *"woe"* to this person and *"woe"* to that person. But when he saw the Lord, his message changed to *"woe is me"* (Is. 6:5). His own sin had to be dealt with before he could get to the place of saying, *"Here am I, send me"* (Is. 6:8).

DURING THE SESSION

 OPENING: 5–10 MINUTES

Opening Prayer—Remember to have one of your group members open your time together in prayer.

Opening Illustration—A good way to begin your discussion time is by asking the question, "Why does a surgeon sterilize his scalpel before he operates?" This should get your group thinking. The main idea they should come to is that a surgeon sterilizes his scalpel to protect his patient from infection. Think about it. A surgeon operating with a dirty scalpel is going to do more harm than good. In fact, he may put the patient's life at risk unnecessarily. The parallel is obvious—God will not use us in someone else's life until He has first cleansed us and made us useable.

⌛ **DISCUSSION: 30–40 MINUTES**

Remember to pace your discussion so that you will be able to bring closure to the lesson in the time allotted. You are the one who must balance lively discussion with timely redirection to ensure that you don't end up finishing only part of the lesson.

Main Objective in Day One: In Day One, the main objective is to see what Isaiah's message was like before his encounter with the Lord. You don't necessarily need to spend a lot of time on Day One, but you want to make sure your group members make the connection that without a clear view of God, it is easy to let the sins of others cloud our view of our own sins. Check which discussion questions from Day One you find to be useful.

_____ What common denominators did you see in Isaiah's early message?

_____ Do you ever struggle with seeing the sins of others more clearly than your own? Why?

_____ Ask your group if they have any questions from their study of Day One.

Main Objective in Day Two: In Day Two, we learn some of the specifics of Isaiah's relationship with King Uzziah and the impact his death may have had on Isaiah's view of himself and of God. The main principle here is that when those around us commit great sins, it is easy to judge our own righteousness by how we "stack up" against them. We will always win such a comparison. Instead, we must realize that sin is not relative—it is not how we are compared to other sinners. Sin is how far we fall short of God. Check which discussion questions from Day Two you will use.

_____ What lessons can we learn from King Uzziah?

_____ How do you think Isaiah felt about the failings of Uzziah?

_____ What effect do you think Uzziah's sin had on Isaiah's view of himself?

_____ How do you think Uzziah's death changed how Isaiah saw himself?

Main Objective in Day Three: Day Three introduces us to the transforming experience Isaiah had when he *"saw the Lord"* (Is. 6:1). There are two key points you want to make sure your group members see from Day Three: **1)** it is God who reveals Isaiah's sin, and **2)** it is God who deals with Isaiah's sin. Isaiah did not see his own sin before, focused as he was on the sins of others. But when he saw the Lord, God revealed to him his own sinfulness. God did not leave him there, though. God only reveals sin so that He can deal with it. Check which discussion questions from Day Three you will use.

_____ Looking at the passage, what things stand out to Isaiah in this vision?

_____ How would you feel if you were in Isaiah's place?

_____ Why do you think Isaiah's lips were touched with fire from the altar?

_____ What else stands out to you from Isaiah's encounter with the Lord?

Main Objective in Day Four: In Day Four, we see the all-important principle that **after** God has dealt with our sin, then He is able to use us. It is on the heels of Isaiah's forgiveness that he receives the invitation from God, "Whom shall I send?" Check which discussion questions from Day Four you will use.

_____ What do you think about the statement, "until we see ourselves as useless, we really aren't useable"?

_____ We usually think of ministry as a "call" (as if God picked us and we had no choice), but here we see it as an "invitation," something to which we can choose to say yes. What do you think about that?

_____ We see that God's task for Isaiah was a ministry with no fruit. Have you ever experienced that?

_____ What kind of struggles did it bring?

Day Five—Key Points in Application: The most important application point out of Day Five is that we cannot use "immediate results" as a yardstick to measure whether or not we are doing what God wants us to do. It is obedience to God, and not results that measure our successes or failures in His work. Check the discussion questions from Day Five that pertain to your study group.

_____ Has a lack of results ever caused you to doubt that you were serving in the right place?

_____ What is the right way to know if you are serving rightly?

_____ Who are the Uzziah's in your life that you measure yourself against?

_____ What is the biggest application point you that you recognized this week?

CLOSING: 5–10 MINUTES

❑ **Summarize**—Highlight the key points.

❑ **Remind** those in your group that the victorious Christian life is not attained when we try hard to be like Jesus, but when we surrender our lives to God and let Him work through us.

❑ **Preview**—Take a few moments to preview next week's lesson on **"Micah: What Does the Lord Require of You."**

❑ **Pray**—Close in prayer.

TOOLS FOR GOOD DISCUSSION

As discussed earlier, there are certain people who show up in every discussion group that you will ever lead. We have already looked at "Talkative Timothy" and "Silent Sally." This week, let's talk about another person who also tends to show up. Let's call this person **"Tangent Tom."** He is the kind of guy who loves to talk even when he has nothing to say. Tangent Tom loves to "chase rabbits" regardless of where they go. When he gets the floor, you never know where the discussion will lead. You need to understand that not all tangents are bad. Sometimes, much can be gained from discussion "a little off the beaten path." But these diversions must be balanced against the purpose of the group. In the "Helpful Hints" section of **How to Lead a Small Group** (p. 6), you will find some practical ideas on managing the "Tangent Tom's" in your group. You will also get some helpful information on evaluating tangents as they arise.

Micah

MEMORY Micah 12:24 VERSE

"He has told you, O man, what is good; and what does the Lord require of you but to do justice, to love kindness, and to walk humbly with your God."

BEFORE THE SESSION

❑ It might be a good idea for you to try to get your homework done early in the week. This will allow time for you to reflect on what you have learned. Don't succumb to the temptation to procrastinate.

❑ Keep a highlight pen handy to highlight any things you want to be sure to discuss or any questions that you think your group may have trouble understanding. Mark down any good discussion questions that come to mind as you study.

❑ If you want to do further study, look at 1 and 2 Kings and 1 and 2 Chronicles, and read about the kings who ruled while Micah ministered. You may also benefit from doing the lesson on **Hezekiah** from *Following God: Life Principles from the Kings of the Old Testament.* The revival of Hezekiah's day was influenced by the ministry of Micah.

❑ Don't think of your ministry to the members of your group as something that only takes place during your group session. Pray for each group member by name during the week. Pray that each member learns much from his or her studies. Encourage all members of your group as you have opportunity.

WHAT TO EXPECT

In this lesson, we are afforded a very practical opportunity to teach our group members the right and wrong ways of dealing with sin. This is one of the most important tools you can place in their spiritual toolboxes. You will make it easier for your members to be open and honest with their own struggles with sin if you come prepared to share from your own experiences and struggles. Knowing that you have not "arrived" spiritually will make it easier for them to face the fact that they have not yet "arrived" and will give them courage to address this important issue.

Our study in Micah will help us focus on what it takes to please God. Micah's message comes as the Northern Kingdom (Israel) faced total annihilation because of that nation's rebellion against Jehovah. God speaks to the Southern Kingdom (Judah) and says, "Even though you are religious, you are just as sinful as rebellious Israel."

> ### THE MAIN POINT
> What God desires from us is not religious ritual, but a heart relationship with Him that produces justice and mercy in our actions.

During the Session

⏳ OPENING: 5–10 MINUTES

Opening Prayer—It would be a good idea to have a different group member open your time together in prayer each week.

Opening Illustration—A good way to begin your discussion time is by asking the question, "What if someone offended you greatly, and instead of apologizing and asking forgiveness, they baked you a plate of cookies—would that make things right in your relationship?" After allowing some discussion, the point you want your group to see is that this is what we do with God when we try to deal with our sins our own way instead of His way.

⏳ DISCUSSION: 30–40 MINUTES

A key objective in how you manage your discussion time is to keep the big picture in view. Your job is not as a school teacher, grading their papers, but as a tutor, making sure they understand the subject. Keep the main point of the lesson in view and make sure they take that point home with them.

Main Objective in Day One: In the discussion for Day One, your main objective as group leader should be to help your group understand the context in which Micah lived and ministered. Nothing is meaningful without a context, and it is impossible to fully appreciate the message and ministry of Micah without understanding the days in which he lived. Since his message is directed to Judah, we will not take the time to study the rulers of the Northern Kingdom during his ministry. Check which discussion questions for Day One that you plan to use.

_____ How do you think the people of Judah viewed the people of the Northern Kingdom (Israel)?

_____ How do you think the people of Judah saw themselves?

_____ How do you think God's judgment of Israel through the Assyrian conquest changed Judah's views?

_____ How do you think Micah's messages changed their views?

_____ What else stood out to you about the days in which Micah ministered?

Main Objective in Day Two: In Day Two, we learn some of the specifics of Micah's message of judgment and his explanations of why it would come. By looking at what he confronts in the people, and by seeing the explanations he gives, we can begin to understand why judgment had come upon Israel, why it would eventually come to Judah, and, in principle, we can see why it comes upon us today. It is important to understand that God judges the sin of His people. As Christians, our eternal destiny with Christ is never to be doubted, but that does not mean that God will not chasten us on earth for our sins. Check which discussion questions you will use from Day Two.

_____ What do you think the people of Judah thought about the idea of God judging them?

_____ On page 100 (workbook), the statement is made that, "A fundamental law of the universe is that we reap what we sow." How do you think that statement applies to Christians?

_____ Why do you think God is so hard on his own people?

_____ Second Timothy 4:3 talks about an inevitable time when people will _"accumulate for themselves teachers in accordance with their own desires."_ What do you think this verse means?

Main Objective in Day Three: Day Three introduces us to the message of hope that accompanied Micah's preaching of judgment. Yes, Judah's sin would have to be addressed. But even though Israel and Judah had changed in how they followed God, Jehovah had not changed in any aspect whatsoever. He would still be faithful to fulfill all that he had promised. God was not (and is still not) finished with Israel. Check the discussion questions that you will use from Day Three.

_____ Do you ever struggle with feeling hopeless when you see your own sin?

_____ What stands out to you as you look at the promises that Micah emphasizes?

_____ Do you expect that God will fulfill all that He has promised to Israel?

_____ Were there any questions raised by your study in Day Three?

Main Objective in Day Four: In Day Four, Micah closes his message to us by drawing our eyes to God's forgiveness and how we are to experience it. Sooner or later, all believers will find themselves in need of a fresh experience of God's forgiveness. Micah shows us how to receive this forgiveness. Check the questions from Day Four that you will use in your discussion

_____ What comes to mind when you hear the word "forgiveness"?

_____ Why do you think forgiveness is still an issue for people who were forgiven at the cross (Christians)?

_____ In Micah 6:6–7, we see some of the ways Israel and Judah tried to make up for their sins. How do we try to do that today?

_____ What should we be doing?

_____ What stands out to you from these last three verses of Micah (7:18-20)?

Day Five—Key Points in Application: The most important application from Day Five is that we cannot approach God on our own terms. We must approach Him as He requires. Micah 6:8 reiterates this thought of coming to God on His terms, and, in reality, we must approach this verse from the end and work our way backward. For example, before we can love mercy with others, and expect justice of ourselves, we must walk humbly with Him. Make sure your group fully understands Micah 6:8. Check which discussion questions from Day Five you will use.

_____ What are some ways we fail to expect justice of ourselves?

_____ What stands out to you about loving mercy in your relationships with others?

_____ What things get in the way of walking humbly with God?

_____ What is the biggest application point you saw this week?

⌛ CLOSING: 5–10 MINUTES

❑ **Summarize**—You may want to read the paragraph at the beginning of the leader's notes for this lesson, called "The Main Point" of Micah.

❑ **Preview**—If time allows, preview next week's lesson, **"Jeremiah: Trusting in God When Life Looks Hopeless."**

❑ **Pray**—Close in prayer.

✂ TOOLS FOR GOOD DISCUSSION 🔨

One of the issues you will eventually have to combat in any group Bible study is the enemy of **boredom.** This antagonist raises its ugly head from time to time, but it shouldn't. It is wrong to bore people with the Word of God! Often boredom results when leaders allow their processes to become too predictable. As small group leaders, we tend to do the same thing in the same way every single time. Yet God the Creator, who spoke everything into existence is infinitely creative! Think about it. He is the one who not only created animals in different shapes and sizes, but different colors as well. When He created food, He didn't make it all taste or feel the same. This God of creativity lives in us. We can trust Him to give us creative ideas that will keep our group times from becoming tired and mundane. In the "Helpful Hints" section of **How to Lead a Small Group** (pp. 8–9), you'll find some practical ideas on adding spice and creativity to your study time.

8

Jeremiah

MEMORY **Psalms 27:13** VERSE

*"I would have despaired unless I had believed that I would
see the goodness of the Lord in the land of the living."*

BEFORE THE SESSION

❑ Your own preparation is key not only to your effectiveness in leading the group-discussion time, but also to your confidence in leading. It is hard to be confident if you know you are unprepared. These discussion questions and leader's notes are meant to be a helpful addition to your own study but should never become a substitute.

❑ As you do your homework, study with an eye to your own relationship with God. Resist the temptation to bypass this self-evaluation on your way to preparing to lead the group. Nothing will minister to your group more than the testimony of your own walk with God.

❑ Look at 1 and 2 Kings and 1 and 2 Chronicles, and read about the kings who ruled while Jeremiah ministered. You may also benefit from doing the lesson on **Josiah** from *Following God: Life Principles from the Kings of the Old Testament.*

❑ Don't think of your ministry to the members of your group as something that only takes place during your group time. Pray for each group member by name during the week, and, as you pray, ask God to enlighten them while they do their homework. Encourage your group as you have opportunity.

WHAT TO EXPECT

In this lesson, we will touch on an area of life that is sometimes painful and vulnerable. It is only fitting that this idea of "trusting God when life looks hopeless" comes later in the study, when relationships have been built to the point of allowing for a certain amount of vulnerability. Be prepared for the possibility that some in your group may be living in a situation that they feel is hopeless, perhaps with an unbelieving spouse or a prodigal child. While these truths from Jeremiah should be a great comfort, they may also bring to the surface some hidden pain. Don't be afraid of some honest emotion spilling out into the group time.

THE MAIN POINT
The main point in Jeremiah is the testimony he offers of faith in God in the midst of hopeless-looking circumstances.

Jeremiah ministered not so much to his own generation, but to the future remnant who would one day return to the promised land. Though he lamented the fall of Jerusalem, he stood on the promises of Jehovah that one day the people of God would return to the land and worship in righteousness. While the story of Jeremiah may seem like ancient history, the principles from his life are just as applicable today when you and I find ourselves in hopeless situations.

DURING THE SESSION

⧖ OPENING: 5–10 MINUTES

Opening Prayer—A good prayer with which to open your time is the prayer of David in Psalms 119:18, *"Open my eyes, that I may behold wonderful things from Thy law."* Remember, if it took the illumination of God for men to write Scripture, it will take the same for us to understand it.

Opening Illustration—A good way to begin your discussion time is by asking the question, "What is the most hopeless situation you can think of?" After allowing some discussion, ask, "Is that situation hopeless for the Christian?" You want your group to understand that usually what is defined as hopeless is based on an earthly, circumstantial set of values instead of being based on an eternal perspective.

⧖ DISCUSSION: 30–40 MINUTES

Remember to pace your discussion so that you don't run out of time to get to the application questions in Day Five. This time for application is perhaps the most important part of your Bible study. It will be helpful if you are familiar enough with the lesson to be able to prioritize the days for which you want to place more emphasis, so that you are prepared to reflect this added emphasis in the time you devote to each day's reading.

Main Objective in Day One: In Day One, the main objective is to understand the context in which Jeremiah lived and ministered. Nothing is meaningful without a context, and it is impossible to fully appreciate the message and ministry of Jeremiah without understanding the days in which he lived. Review the discussion questions for Day One below, and check the ones that you will use for your discussion time:

_____ What stands out to you about the last four kings of Judah?

_____ What were the three things God did to Jeremiah before He formed him in the womb?

_____ How do those three things apply to us today?

_____ Have you ever felt "too young" for a responsibility God has given you? What does Jeremiah have to say about that?

Main Objective in Day Two: In Day Two, we learn some of the specifics of Jeremiah's preaching. By looking at what he confronts in the people, and by seeing the response for which he calls from them, we can have a sense of what God desires from His people throughout the ages. It is important to understand that God judges the sin of His people. Though we may be Christians who are eternally saved by God's grace, He will still chasten us for our transgressions. Check which discussion questions you will use from Day Two.

_____ The two sins of Judah were **a)** forsaking the fountain of living waters (God), and **b)** hewing their own cisterns that would hold no water. What are some ways people do that today?

_____ In speaking of their judgment, Jeremiah 2:19 says, *"Your own wickedness will correct you."* Can you think of some examples from your life or those you know where sin was its own punishment?

_____ How do we distinguish true repentance over sin from remorse over sin's consequences?

_____ What else stood out to you from Day Two?

Main Objective in Day Three: Day Three introduces us to the pain of speaking truth to those who reject it. Jeremiah's was not a pleasant ministry. His example ought to remind us that we do not judge the success or failure of a ministry or task based on how people respond, but rather, based on being faithful to God's assignment. Check the questions below from Day Three that you find to be essential to your group's discussion.

_____ Jeremiah was faithful to preach truth even though he had no expectation that the people would respond. How does Jeremiah's faithfulness apply to us today?

_____ Have you ever experienced grief like that of Jeremiah's over someone else who vehemently refused to repent?

_____ What are some modern examples of persecution to those who preach truth?

_____ Why do you think the unrepentant persecute the messenger when they hear truth?

_____ Were there any questions raised by your study in Day Three?

Main Objective in Day Four: In Day Four, our study of Jeremiah takes us to the reality that, sooner or later, God will place us in a situation where we have to act in faith instead of by sight. He will call us to step out on truth instead of allowing us to react to our circumstances. Jeremiah also shows us the necessity of keeping our future hope in view as we face the present. Check the discussion questions from Day Four that you will use in your group session.

_____ What stands out to you from this story of Jeremiah buying the farm?

_____ Have you ever experienced "buyer's remorse" after stepping out in faith?

_____ What do you learn from the future promises made to Israel?

_____ What are some ways our present life on earth requires walking by faith rather than walking by sight?

_____ What else stood out to you from Day Four?

Day Five—Key Points in Application: Among the applications introduced in Day Five, the most noteworthy concept is that we should not be as concerned with the visible results of our actions as in whether or not we are doing what God has called us to do. Make sure that your group understands that success in life always comes in doing what God says and leaving the results to Him. Check any questions that you would like to use for discussion on Day Five.

_____ Of the three things God did before He formed Jeremiah (_"knew," "consecrated," "appointed"_ [Jeremiah 1:5]), which stands out the most to you personally?

_____ Is there a hopeless situation in your life you need to surrender to God? Do you need to accept what He has appointed for you?

_____ Out of fear, have you failed to do something that you know God has called you to?

_____ Is there anything you need to "recall to mind" about God in your present circumstances?

_____ What other applications did you come to understand from this week's lesson?

⧖ CLOSING: 5–10 MINUTES

❑ **Summarize**—Restate the key points. You may want to read the paragraph at the beginning of the leader's notes for Jeremiah called "The Main Point."

❑ **Preview**—If time allows, preview next week's lesson on **"Habakkuk: Following God in the Low Places of Life."**

❑ **Pray**—Close in prayer.

Tools for Good Discussion

From time to time each of us can say stupid things. Some of us, however, are better at it than others. I suspect the apostle Peter fell into this category. One minute he was on the pinnacle of success saying, _"Thou art the Christ, the Son of the Living God"_ (Matthew 16:16), and the next minute he was putting his foot in his mouth, trying to talk Jesus out of going to the cross. Proverbs 10:19 states, _"When there are many words, transgression is unavoidable. . . ."_ What do you do when someone in the group says something that is obviously wrong? First of all, remember that how you deal with a situation like this not only affects the present, but the future. In the "Helpful Hints" section of **How to Lead a Small Group Bible Study** (p. 9), you'll find some practical ideas on managing the obviously mistaken comments that may be presented in your group discussion.

9

Habakkuk

MEMORY **Habakkuk 3:18–19** VERSES

"Yet I will exult in the Lord, I will rejoice in the God of my salvation. The Lord God is my strength, And He . . . makes me walk on my high places."

BEFORE THE SESSION

❑ Pray each day for the members of your group—that they spend time in the Word, grasp the message God wants to bring to their lives, and that they surrender to what God is saying to them through their study of His Word.

❑ As you pray that your group members will grow in their study of the Scriptures, make sure you have searched the Scriptures carefully for each day's lesson as well.

❑ Walk through the discussion questions given throughout this Leader's Guide lesson, and select which questions you think might enhance your group discussion.

❑ **Suggestions for Additional Study**—To better understand the condition of Judah at this time you may want to review last week's lesson on **Jeremiah,** and look at *Following God: Life Principles from the Kings of the Old Testament,* (Lesson 9), entitled **"Josiah: The Impact of Following the Word of God."**

❑ Remain ever teachable. Look first for what God is saying to you. This will help you in understanding and relating to some of the struggles that your group members may be facing in the "low places" they are going through.

WHAT TO EXPECT

This lesson may reveal some evident struggles that one or a few members of your group may be facing. Do not feel like you have to be "The Answer Man" or "The Answer Woman." Sometimes the most faith-filled response to a question is "I don't know," followed by "but we know we can trust God. He is faithful and trustworthy." Some in your group will have some tremendous testimonies of victory or rejoicing in the midst of some very dark days. You may see and hear some wonderful testimonies of the grace of God at work. I knew a very dear man of God, Oscar Thompson, a professor of evangelism at Southwestern Seminary in Fort Worth, Texas in the 1970's. The ravaging effects of cancer plagued his body, and he faced some very rough days before his death. But he also experienced some wonderful days of grace. God allowed him to minister and counsel many people from all over the country who were facing the pains of chemotherapy or even the day of their death. He often spoke to them of the grace of God. He said, "God gives dying grace on dying days." He does not give dying grace on non-dying days. Oscar Thompson lived in that reality and died in that reality. God truly gives whatever grace and wisdom we need when we need it. Help your group members see this truth so that they may continue to follow God through the low places of their lives.

THE MAIN POINT

We will learn to live by faith in the "high places" of God's grace, as we walk through the "low places" of the dark circumstances in life.

DURING THE SESSION

 OPENING: 5–10 MINUTES

Opening Prayer—Remember to ask the Lord for **His** wisdom. He promised to guide us into the truth.

Opening Illustration—The following hymn, "He Giveth More Grace" was written by Annie Johnson Flint:

"He giveth more grace when the burden grows greater;
He sendeth more strength when the labors increase.
To added affliction He addeth His mercy;
to multiplied trials, His multiplied peace.

"His love has no limit; His grace has no measure;
His pow'r has no boundary known unto men.
For out of His infinite riches in Jesus,
He giveth, and giveth, and giveth again!"

The second verse says,

"When we have exhausted our store of endurance,
When our strength has failed ere the day is half done,
When we reach the end of our hoarded resources,
Our Father's full giving is only begun."

["He Giveth More Grace" © 1941, Renewed 1969 Lillenas Publishing Co. Used by permission]

How true these words are for the trials we face!

 DISCUSSION: 30–40 MINUTES

Select one or two specific questions to get the group started. Keep the group focused along the main study of Habakkuk. By this point in the course (Week 9), you know both the talkative ones and the quiet ones. Continue to encourage members in the importance of their input. Some of the greatest life lessons we ever learn may come from someone who has said very little up to this point.

Main Objective in Day One: In Day One, the main objective is to see the symptoms of being in a "low place," the darkness and distress sin has brought. Check the discussion questions for Day One that you will use.

_____ What was the condition of Judah in the days of Habakkuk, especially around 609–605 B.C.? What parallels do you see today?

_____ How does a leader affect those around him? What did you discover about King Jehoahaz?

_____ How do the sins of others bring discouragement to you personally? What can we do to encourage one another to follow the Lord and obey His Word day-by-day?

_____ How do you face the questions you have (especially the unanswered questions) about the way circumstances are turning out for you? How could you help others with their particular questions?

Main Objective in Day Two: Here we learn that the "low places" show us our hearts and our attitudes, especially the attitude of **pride**. Make sure everyone in your group sees the truth about pride in today's lesson. Check the discussion questions for Day Two that you will use.

_____ What is the difference between living by sight (feelings, emotions, human logic) and living by faith (God's logic)? You may want to read 2 Corinthians 4:16–18, the testimony of Paul in the face of the pressure of circumstances.

_____ Describe pride. What does a prideful person look like, sound like, act like?

_____ How has God dealt with you about an area of pride? Can you recall a time when God was speaking specifically to you about your pride?

_____ What are some ways we try to fix circumstances in others' lives or in our own instead of urging others to humble themselves before God or humbling ourselves before God?

_____ What are some ways God may seek to bring us to humble ourselves?

Main Objective in Day Three: In Day Three, the study concentrates on Habakkuk's new attitude toward God. Select a question or two from the list below that you think might be useful for your discussion of Day Three.

_____ Habakkuk truly heard the message that God spoke to him. What are some ways God speaks in the midst of our circumstances?

_____ How can we make sure we are "all ears" when God is speaking?

_____ How can we gain a clearer view of who God is and what He wants in our lives?

_____ What are some ways God has worked in your life, both to your benefit and to the benefit of others around you?

_____ Are there some things God has revealed about Himself that you would not have known had it not been for the rough days that God has allowed to enter your life?

Main Objective in Day Four: Here we see the triumph of Habakkuk in the midst of the coming calamities of his people. His focus was on the Lord and how the Lord would guide His people **through** the difficult days. Check a question or two from the list below that you find to be profitable to your discussion of Day Four.

_____ Habakkuk trembled when he thought about what the future held. Yet, he also rejoiced. How do the ideas of trembling and rejoicing fit together?

_____ How can a person have joy even in the midst of difficulties, including the loss of prosperity? What was Habakkuk's solution to all that he faced?

_____ How can you personally focus more fully on the Lord, and how can you help others do the same?

Day Five—Key Points in Application: The most noteworthy application point from Day Five is that we make sure that our faith is directed upon God, not on people or earthly things. Encourage your group members to discern whether the motivations for their lifestyles come from God or from the world. Review the Day Five question list below, and select the ones that you feel will enhance your group discussion.

_____ What shapes the way most people (even many Christians) look at life?

_____ What do you know for sure about God's knowledge and wisdom? What are some

world opinions that have gotten mixed in with what you see in Scripture?

_____ How has God shown His love in your life?

_____ What are some struggles you have faced, difficulties that are dark threads in the tapestry that God is weaving? What is God saying to you through Habakkuk?

⧖ CLOSING: 5–10 MINUTES

❏ **Summarize**—Restate the key points the group shared. Review the objectives for each of the days found at the beginning of these leader notes.

❏ **Focus**—Using the memory verses (Habakkuk 3:18–19), focus the group on the centrality of faith in the character and ways of God. As Psalm 119:68 says, _"Thou art good and doest good."_ We can trust Him.

❏ **Ask** them to share their thoughts concerning Day Five, especially the truths about the "gates" that all God's decisions come through.

❏ **Encourage**—We have finished nine lessons. This is no time to slack off. Encourage your group to keep up the pace. We have three more lessons full of life-changing truths. Take a few moments to preview next week's lesson on **"Daniel: Confidence in the God of Heaven."** Encourage your group members to do their homework and to space it out over the week.

❏ Close in prayer.

TOOLS FOR GOOD DISCUSSION

The Scriptures are full of examples of people who struggled with the problem of pride. Unfortunately, pride isn't a problem reserved for the history books. It shows up just as often today as it did in the days the Scriptures were written. In your group discussions, you may see traces of pride manifested in a "know-it-all" group member. **"Know-It-All Ned"** may have shown up in your group by this point. He may be an intellectual giant, or he may be a legend only in his own mind. He can be very prideful and argumentative. If you want some helpful hints on how to deal with "Know-It-All Ned," look in the "Helpful Hints" section of **How to Lead a Small Group Bible Study** (p. 7).

10

Daniel

MEMORY **Isaiah 66:2b** VERSE

*"But to this one will I look, to him who is humble and contrite
of spirit, and who trembles at My word."*

BEFORE THE SESSION

❏ Never underestimate the importance of prayer for yourself and for the members of your group. Ask the Lord to give them understanding in their time in the Word and bring them to a new level of knowing Him.

❏ Remember to mark those ideas and questions you want to discuss or ask as you go through the study.

❏ Suggestions for Additional Study: To better understand the condition of Judah at this time you may want to look at two lessons in *Following God: Life Principles from the Kings of the Old Testament*. The first lesson is titled, **"Josiah: The Impact of Following the Word of God."** To see how God worked near the end of Daniel's life you may want to look at **"Zerubbabel and Ezra: Following God's Will."**

❏ Be sensitive to the needs of your group. Be prepared to stop and pray for a member who may be facing a difficult struggle or challenge.

WHAT TO EXPECT

Some in your group may recall some things they have heard about Daniel as a youth (i.e., the story of Daniel in the Lion's Den), while others may find the study completely new. There may be some tough questions that surface in dealing with the things God allows in our lives or in facing some matters dealing with authorities in our lives. Remember that your job is not to teach the lesson, but to guide discussion so that all can learn from each other. You will want to emphasize the faithfulness of God in Daniel's life and how God is ever faithful to each member in your group. Just because God is always faithful to us does not mean that He will reveal to us all of the why's and why not's of life. God's faithfulness to us means that He will take us all the way to the finish line in the race He has set out for us. He takes us there in His way, in His timing, along His paths. Those paths are always chosen out of His covenant love for us, and He has promised to **never** leave us nor forsake us—just as we see in Daniel's life. May this lesson be a real encouragement to your group to **see God** at work in their lives and to **seek God** in the circumstances they are facing.

THE MAIN POINT
We can place our total confidence and trust in the God of Heaven who rules over all. He is **always** at work fulfilling His purposes for His people.

During the Session

OPENING: 5–10 MINUTES

Opening Prayer—Have one of the group members open the time with prayer.

Opening Illustration—Confidence in the Word of God. King Josiah emphasized the importance of following **all** of the Word of God (2 Kings 23:25). Apparently he made an impact on young Daniel and Daniel's family. The Babylonian army was known for its fierce and proud soldiers. Their reputation had spread far and wide. Habakkuk had talked much about them. Now Daniel faced them and was a captive in their caravan back to Babylon. As a fourteen-year-old youth he discovered that the Word of God was sufficient wherever he was and in whatever circumstance he faced. His confidence in the God of Heaven meant a confidence in the Word of the God of Heaven. We can discover the same.

DISCUSSION: 30–40 MINUTES

Select one or two specific questions to get the group to start talking. This lesson on Daniel covers over 70 years of his life and has application points for every stage of life. Focus on the power and reign of the Lord in our lives. Keep the group directed on the **faithfulness of God** in Daniel's life as well as on the **faith of Daniel** in God's faithfulness. Continue to encourage each member in the importance of his or her input.

Main Objective in Day One: In Day One the main objective is to see the righteous God Daniel knew and Daniel's desire to follow His righteous Word. Check which discussion questions you will use from Day One .

_____ What would it mean to have a king like Josiah leading the people (imagine you and your parents) in following all the Word of God? How would you respond if you were Daniel?

_____ What would it be like to hear about coming judgment and then see the armies of Babylon? If you were Daniel's parents, what would you say to your children when you heard Habakkuk, Jeremiah, or Zephaniah proclaiming the message God had given

him? How would you prepare yourself or your children in light of the messages of these prophets?

_____ How do you face new circumstances? Think of all the "new" things Daniel and his friends faced. Have you experienced a major move with your family or some major change in your life? What can you learn from Daniel about what's important?

_____ Sometimes we must take a stand or confront a person or group because of a personal conviction God has given us. What principles have you gleaned from the way Daniel responded to his situation?

Main Objective in Day Two: Sometimes we face situations that are beyond our own understanding or abilities, but they are not beyond God's. The Lord wants us to depend on Him and look to Him for His wisdom and grace for difficult situations. Check the discussion questions that you will use from Day Two.

_____ What stood out to you about Daniel's attitude and confidence in God in the face of this trial?

_____ What were priorities to Daniel and his three friends? What did they do first? second? third? What does that say to you about how you should face trials?

_____ Can you think of a time when you faced a trial in which you needed wisdom, and how God gave you that wisdom?

_____ Describe a time when you depended on man's wisdom, man's might or strength, or man's riches. What did God teach you (or what is He teaching you now about this) in light of Jeremiah 9:23–24?

_____ What practical lessons can you glean from Daniel's confidence in God's ability to reveal the way to go, the choices to make, and the things to do? What about the things **not** to do?

Main Objective in Day Three: The main objective is to see that _"it is Heaven that rules"_ and in seeing that to also see the attitude of humility and trust that God wants in us. Check the discussion questions from Day Three that are relevant to your group.

_____ Nebuchadnezzar's dream was followed by twelve months of waiting. God was waiting to see his response, then He acted to carry out the dream He had given him. How have you seen the Lord's reign in your life through His timing of some event or answer to prayer?

_____ Nebuchadnezzar's view of life was filled with pride. What are some ways that **pride** fills our view of life today? What do we need to do when we see this?

_____ What are some ways God has humbled you in your pride?

_____ Daniel served for many years under several rulers, some of whom were very proud. How did Daniel serve under such men? Where was his focus, and how did that focus get him through those years of service?

Main Objective in Day Four: Daniel's relationship with the Lord impacted all that he did—his job and his home life, not just his spiritual life. The same can be true of us. Place a check mark near the questions that are best suited for your discussion.

_____ Daniel was marked by integrity on the job. How important is integrity? What difference did Daniel's integrity make to Darius or to Daniel's co-workers?

_____ How can our relationship to God affect our relationships to those in authority over us? How can our relationships with those in authority over us affect our fellowship with God?

_____ How important is the Word of God in our lives? In Daniel 9, we find that Daniel was reading the prophecy of Jeremiah. How do you think that affected how he prayed and what he prayed?

_____ Where was Daniel focused as he thought of and prayed for Jerusalem and the people of Israel? How does that speak to you about your focus in life or your focus in prayer?

Day Five—Key Points in Application: The most important application point seen in the life of Daniel is this: we should make sure that we see life and its many circumstances from **God's point of view** rather than seeing life only from the level of our cir-

cumstances. Check which discussion questions you will use from Day Five.

_____ In God's scheme of things, how we finish the race is far more important than how we start the race. How did Daniel finish his race? What can you do to insure a good finish in your life?

_____ Daniel served under a variety of authorities—some idolatrous, some proud, some unpredictable. Paul the Apostle wrote Romans 13 (about authorities) during the reign of Nero, a very wicked ruler.

_____ Where was the focus of Daniel or Paul? How did they deal with authorities in their lives? What can we learn from them?

_____ What has God shown you about the "kingdom" where you are "ruling" or, in most cases, serving?

_____ Daniel has some things to say about facing surprises in life. What do we know for sure about the surprises of life, things like sudden changes in our jobs, schools, locations, finances, relationships, friends or family?

⌛ CLOSING: 5–10 MINUTES

❏ **Summarize.**

❏ **Ask** your group to express their thoughts about the key applications from Day Five.

❏ **Preview**—Take time to preview next week's lesson, **"Haggai: A Call to Consider Your Ways."**

❏ **Pray**—Close in prayer.

TOOLS FOR GOOD DISCUSSION

So, group leaders, how have the first nine weeks of this study been for you? Have you dealt with anyone in your group called **"Agenda Alice"**? She is the type that is focused on a Christian "hot-button" issue instead of the Bible study. If not managed properly, she (or he) will either sidetrack the group from its main study objective, or create a hostile environment in the group if she fails to bring people to her way of thinking. For help with "Agenda Alice," see the "Helpful Hints" section of **How to Lead a Small Group Bible Study** (pp. 7–8).

11

Haggai

MEMORY **2 Corinthians 6:16** VERSE

"For we are the temple of the living God; just as God said, 'I will dwell in them and walk among them; and I will be their God, and they shall by My people.'"

BEFORE THE SESSION

❏ Pray for your group as they walk through this week's lesson.

❏ Spread your study time over the week. Think of the lesson as a large meal. You need time to chew each truth and digest it fully.

❏ Remember to mark those ideas and questions you want to discuss or ask as you go.

❏ For additional study, you can better understand the condition of Jerusalem at the time of Zerubbabel by looking at the lesson, **"Zerubbabel and Ezra: Following God's Will"** (Lesson 10) in *Following God: Life Principles from the Kings of the Old Testament.*

WHAT TO EXPECT

Haggai will be a new name for some (perhaps for all) in your group. He appears only for a brief moment on the stage of the Old Testament, but what He said lingers throughout time into eternity. Along with the newness of Haggai, some will find the discussion about the Tabernacle or Temple to be new or at least unfamiliar. There may be a few questions about Zerubbabel or the "signet ring" or God's promises for the future that are not easily answered.

Be patient. Study diligently in your preparation time. You may want to consult a Bible dictionary about some of these things. As you tread through the lesson, seek to keep the main point the main point. Emphasize what you clearly know and understand. Then you can move on to the things that are not as clear as the Lord gives time and insight.

> ### THE MAIN POINT
> God continually calls us to "consider" our "ways" in our walk with Him, and He calls us to adjust our ways to His ways through following His Word.

DURING THE SESSION

⏳ **OPENING: 5–10 MINUTES**

Opening Prayer—Have one of the group members open the time with prayer.

Opening Illustration—It's the Little Things That Count. Often we are tempted to think that only the big things in life, or the big events, or the "big name" people are what is really important. But a small rudder turns the greatest of ships, and the tongue, though it is one of the smallest members of our bodies, is often the most powerful. How many times we have found that it is not a whole book or a whole chapter of the Bible that impacts—but a small verse or part of a verse or phrase empowered by the Spirit of God that pierces us in soul and spirit. This little book of Haggai (only two chapters, 38 verses) has this powerful potential. In this small book, the call to consider our ways rings clear with the promise that obedience will bring the blessing of God.

⧗ DISCUSSION: 30–40 MINUTES

This lesson on Haggai covers only a year of his life but looks at God's plans for the ages. Focus on the Lord's call to consider our ways in the light of His plans in our lives. Keep the group directed at the mercy and faithfulness of God. Help them see His "never give up" attitude with His people and with His plans. Every **call** for us to consider our ways is a **promise** that His mercy and grace are available to the obedient heart.

Main Objective in Day One: The main point here is to discover the preeminence of God's priorities and the importance of making those priorities ours. Check which discussion questions you will use from Day One.

_____ Do you find it easy to focus on "taking care of business" (i.e., your own "business") and forgetting the things of God?

_____ What things got in the way of building the Temple in Haggai's day? What things can get in the way of what God wants to do in and through our lives?

_____ How can we follow the command to "set your heart on your ways"? How do we "set" our hearts or "consider" our ways?

_____ God got their attention through their economy (the dew, the crops, and their expenses). How does the Lord get our attention today? How has he gotten your attention about your walk?

Main Objective in Day Two: In Day Two, we learn the importance of God's presence and what it means to walk practicing His presence. Check the discussion questions for Day Two that you will use.

_____ How have you seen the difference between "existing" and "living" in your life or perhaps in your family's life?

_____ What does it mean to you that God wants to "dwell with" **you**?

_____ What does "fearing the Lord" mean to you? What are some ways you can (or do) show reverence for the Lord?

_____ We see that the people of Jerusalem were energized by their obedience to the Word of the Lord. What does it mean to be "energized" by your obedience? What does that look like?

Main Objective in Day Three: Day Three focuses on the promise of the presence and provision of the Lord as the people obeyed. Decide which discussion questions for Day Three you will use from the list below:

_____ What would the promise of the Lord's presence and provision mean to people walking out of Egypt into the Wilderness of Sinai? What would it mean to people rebuilding a temple from the rubble in a city with no walls and a depressed economy?

_____ What is the one thing someone wants when they are really thirsty? What kind of thirst did Jesus talk about in John 7? Name some ways you have experienced thirst—physically or spiritually.

_____ Name some ways Jesus has quenched your soul's thirst. What is the difference between the **"living water"** Jesus gives and the "waters" of the world?

_____ Haggai's messages were meant to bring the people into a much greater understanding and experience of the presence and provision of God in daily life. What do the promises of God mean in your life today? How do the promises of God give you comfort or encouragement?

Main Objective in Day Four: Day Four looks at how the Lord treated Israel to bring them back to a full experience of His presence and power. Check which discussion questions you will use from Day Four.

_____ **Whatever It Takes**—That is what we see again and again as Haggai speaks (Haggai 2:16–17) about how God uses different means to get our attention, to cause us to look up to Him in a fresh way, to come to a new day of full obedience. What does this tell you about the Lord?

____ The Lord not only used circumstances to speak to His people, He also sent His prophets with a clear message from His heart. God speaks through His Word to us today. What hinders us from obeying what is clear in His Word?

____ All that God did and said was meant to encourage and energize His people in their walk and for the tasks they would face in the days ahead. How can you be an encouragement and an energizer to others as opposed to a "discourager" and an "energy-drainer"?

____ The Lord did not stop His words of encouragement to Haggai. He had more to say through Zechariah. What does this tell you about the Lord's love and care for His people? What does this say about His care for you today? How can this encourage you and others in following God?

Day Five—Key Points in Application: The most important application point seen in the ministry of Haggai is found in the statement: *"consider your ways"* (Haggai 1:5). Is He real in the everyday affairs of your life, or do you just give Him a little attention on Sunday? Check which discussion questions from Day Five you will use.

____ We don't go to a Temple to acknowledge the presence of the Lord, we are the Temple of His Spirit. Everywhere we go, God and His Temple goes. How can the recognition of the truth that we are the Temple of God's Spirit affect your daily life?

____ What has this lesson said to you about your priorities? Are they the priorities that a disciple of Jesus Christ should have?

____ On page 179 in the workbook, the statement is made: "He wants us to walk—not **ahead** of Him, trying to control our own lives; not **behind** Him, rebelling against Him and His ways; but **with** Him, cooperating and enjoying the fellowship of the journey." What are some application points in that statement that touch your life?

____ God speaks in a language we understand. He uses the image of a tent to speak of dwelling with His people, of living with them like a family. Think of some pictures that describe the kind of relationship God wants with you (for example, a Father to a child).

⏳ CLOSING: 5–10 MINUTES

❑ **Summarize**—Restate the key points.

❑ **Ask** the group members to share their thoughts about the key applications from Day Five.

❑ **Preview**—Take time to preview next week's lesson on **"Christ the Prophet: Worshiping in Spirit and Truth."** Encourage them to do their homework for this final lesson in the study of the Old Testament prophets.

❑ **Pray**—Close in prayer.

TOOLS FOR GOOD DISCUSSION

Well, it is evaluation time again! You may be saying to yourself, "Why bother evaluating at the end? If I did a bad job, it is too late to do anything about it now!" Well, it may be too late to change how you did on this course, but it is never too late to learn from this course what will help you on the next. Howard Hendricks, that peerless communicator from Dallas Theological Seminary, puts it this way: "The good teacher's greatest threat is satisfaction—the failure to keep asking, 'How can I improve?' The greatest threat to your ministry is **your ministry.**" Any self-examination should be an accounting of your own strengths and weaknesses. As you consider your strengths and weaknesses, take some time to read through the evaluation questions list found in the **How to Lead a Small Group Bible Study** section on pages 11–12 of this leader's guide. Make it your aim to continue growing as a discussion leader. Below, jot down two or three action points for you to implement in future classes.

ACTION POINTS:

1. _____

_____

2. _____

_____

3. _____

_____

12

Christ the Prophet

MEMORY **John 5:24** VERSE

"Truly, truly, I say to you, he who hears My word, and believes Him who sent Me, has eternal life, and does not come into judgment, but has passed out of death into life."

BEFORE THE SESSION

❑ Never underestimate the importance of prayer for yourself and for the members of your group. Pray for each group member by name.

❑ Spread your study time over the week.

❑ Remember to mark those ideas and questions you want to discuss or ask as you go through the study. Add to those some of the questions listed below.

❑ Be sensitive to the working of the Spirit in your group meeting, ever watchful for ways to help one another truly follow God.

WHAT TO EXPECT

Like seeing the facets of a diamond or emerald from several angles, seeing Christ as The Prophet will hopefully give fresh perspective to the members in your group. Hopefully, all will experience a deeper level of obedience to the Lord and His Word, and with that, discover the reward of receiving a prophet (The Prophet) of the Lord. When we focus on Jesus Christ we often discover answers to the deepest cries of our heart. We also face new questions and desire greater understanding. Some questions may arise that you may not be able to answer

or to answer as fully as you would like. Remember that you do not need to be "The Answer Man" or "The Answer Woman" for all the things that come up. Rejoice in the new insights and challenge the group to deeper study with the unknowns. As you move through the lesson, seek to keep the main focus the main focus. Emphasize what you clearly know and understand. Then you can move on to the things that are not as clear as the Lord gives time and insight.

THE MAIN POINT

As we study the life and ministry of Christ Jesus the Prophet, we will learn the necessity of honoring Him and His Word with a life of worship in spirit (heart) and truth.

DURING THE SESSION

⏳ **OPENING: 5–10 MINUTES**

Opening Prayer—Psalm 119:18 says, *"Open my eyes, that I may behold wonderful things from Thy law."* Ask the Lord to open your eyes as you meet together. Have one of the group members open the time with prayer.

Opening Illustration—It has been said of George Whitefield, the great evangelist of the First Great

Awakening (1740s), that he could be clearly heard in a crowd of 20,000 with no means of amplification. More than that, his message thundered with the conviction of the Holy Spirit through the hearts of thousands. Imagine what it was like to hear the Lord Jesus when He spoke His Sermon on the Mount or when He spoke at the feeding of the 5,000. Matthew 7:28–29 says *"the multitudes were amazed at His teaching; for He was teaching them as one having authority, and not as their scribes."* As you look at Christ the Prophet, may He speak with authority and conviction to each one in your group.

⧗ DISCUSSION: 30–40 MINUTES

This lesson on Christ the Prophet focuses on Christ's clear grasp of the Word of His Father, how He faithfully proclaimed that Word, and the reward for an obedient response on the part of His hearers. For today, through this lesson, **we** are each His hearers. The admonition of Hebrews 12:1–2 cries out to all of us, *". . . let us run with endurance the race that is set before us,* **fixing our eyes on Jesus,** *the author and perfecter of faith. . . ."* As you and your group set your eyes on Christ the Prophet, hearing and heeding His Word will result in a greater walk of faith and a deeper experience of His joy.

Main Objective in Day One: The main point here is to see how the Lord raises up those who speak the truth because He longs for His people to walk in that truth. Ultimately, He sent His Son, the Lord Jesus. Choose one or more discussion questions from Day One that is relevant to your group.

_____ God warned about deception and lies in the Canaanite culture. What are some of the sources of falsehood, lies, and deception we face in our lives today?

_____ How does the fact that God wants you to know the truth bring encouragement to you? What are some of His sources of truth for us today?

_____ How important is it to come to the Lord and His Word with an open, listening heart? How can we do that more consistently?

_____ Have you ever heard someone speak "straw" as opposed to "grain," like Jeremiah talked about? How have you seen the difference in your life or in what you have heard?

Main Objective in Day Two: In Day Two, the main objective is to see how Christ fulfilled the promise given to Moses—God would raise up a prophet like Moses who would speak **all** the Word He gave Him to speak. Check the questions that you might consider using for your group discussion for Day Two.

_____ What would it be like to know that the one teaching you was absolutely true in everything he said? What do you think the people thought as they heard Jesus?

_____ What is it like when you learn that someone has told you something that was deceptive in any way?

_____ Jesus spoke with authority. How does your confidence in the Lord Jesus and His Word bring comfort or encouragement to you?

_____ Jesus had an open, honest relationship with His Father. He walked in the freedom of the truth. How has His truth given you freedom in some area?

Main Objective in Day Three: Day Three focuses on **the focus** of the Lord Jesus—a right relationship with God the Father and right worship. Check the discussion questions that you will use for Day Three.

_____ What are some things that get in the way of people seeing God as He really is? Or to put it another way: What are some of the substitutes for true worship? With what do people try to replace true worship?

_____ How do Christians sometimes fail to worship in spirit and truth? What gets in the way in their relationship with God the Father?

_____ Why does the Lord want us to deal honestly with our sin? What good is that? How important is that?

_____ What is the result of dealing with sin and focusing on pure worship in spirit and truth?

Main Objective in Day Four: Day Four looks at the importance of receiving The Prophet and the message He brings. Check which discussion questions from Day Four you will use.

_____ Many believed Jesus to be a prophet, but refused to heed what He said. What does it mean to receive Him and His Word?

_____ A personal relationship with Jesus Christ involves walking with Him in the truth. What should we do when we do not fully understand Him or His Word?

_____ Practically speaking, how do we continue receiving His Word?

_____ What has it meant to you to receive Jesus Christ as your Lord and Savior, as the Prophet, the Way, the Truth, and the Life?

Day Five—Key Points in Application: The most important application point in the study of Christ the Prophet is the practical application of His Word to our lives. Place a checkmark next to the questions for Day Two that you will use in your discussion time.

_____ What can you do to insure that you are continuing to hear Christ the Prophet?

_____ Is there an area where you are struggling, where there is little or no freedom, where you don't know the truth that deals with that struggle?

_____ What are you doing to prepare for His prophesied return?

_____ What has the Lord showed you about your worship and obedience of Him?

⧖ CLOSING: 5–10 MINUTES

❑ **Summarize**—Restate the key points.

❑ **Focus**—Using the memory verse (John 5:24), focus the group on what it means to truly hear and believe His Word.

❑ **Ask** some of your group members to share their thoughts about the key applications from Day Five.

❑ **Pray**—Close your time in prayer by thanking the Lord for the journey of learning on which He has led you over the past 12 weeks.

TOOLS FOR GOOD DISCUSSION

Congratulations! You have successfully navigated the waters of small group discussion. You have finished all 12 lessons in _Following God: Life Principles from the Prophets of the Old Testament_, but there is so much more to learn, so many more paths to take on our journey with the Lord, so much more to discover about what it means to follow Him. Now What? It may be wise for you and your group to continue with another study. In the front portion of this leader's guide (in the "Helpful Hints" section of **How to Lead a Small Group Bible Study,** pp. 9–10), there is information on how you can transition to the next study and share those insights with your group. Encourage your group to continue in some sort of consistent Bible study. Time in the Word is much like time at the dinner table. If we are to stay healthy, we will never get far from physical food, and if we are to stay nourished on "sound" or "healthy" doctrine, then we must stay close to the Lord's "dinner table" found in His Word. Job said it well, _"I have not departed from the command of His lips; I have treasured the words of His mouth more than my necessary food"_ (Job 23:12).